Nooma

May the fox
be with you!

Chris Jones

Chantell Ilbury / Clem Sunter

Socrates & the FOX

A Strategic Dialogue

HUMAN & ROUSSEAU / TAFELBERG

Published jointly by Human & Rousseau
and Tafelberg, both imprints of
NB Publishers,
40 Heerengracht, Cape Town

Cover design by Jürgen Fomm
Text designed and typeset in 11.5 on 14 pt Palatino
by Nazli Jacobs
Printed and bound by Paarl Print, Oosterland Street, Paarl
South Africa

First edition, first impression November 2007
Second impression September 2008
Third impression January 2009
Fourth impression July 2009
Fifth impression September 2009

ISBN: 978-0-7981-4905-1

THIS BOOK IS DEDICATED TO

Our families who are our foundation;
Our friends who stand by us in good and bad times;
Our colleagues who assisted in producing the book in
   such a professional manner;
Margaret Berry;
and
The fox within you – whoever you are, wherever
   you are and whatever you do.

Contents

PROLOGUE

1 Socrates: A Brief History

The highest form of human excellence is to question oneself and others.
SOCRATES

"You are a traitor and deserve to die. And it shall be by your own hand."

Suppose you received an e-mail to this effect from your boss because you had dared to question his judgment on a strategic issue, and had persuaded some of your junior colleagues of the validity of your case. At the very least, you would consider his reaction to be over the top and ask for his decision to be reviewed by the human resources department. Yet this was the opinion of a public court of Athens that found the wisest man in Greece and the father of Western philosophy guilty of heresy and corrupting the youth. He posed an unacceptable threat to his Athenian bosses with his weapon of mass deduction: Socratic dialogue.

Yes, we are talking about Socrates. At the time of his death (399 BC), the once mighty Athenian Empire was recovering from defeat by Sparta following a destructive and protracted war between the two neighbouring Greek states. Socrates was highly critical of the Athenian strategy and debated the merits of alternatives with his students, many of them young aristocrats, and one of them Plato. He thus became the focus of the ire of a number of leading public figures. They declared that not only was he openly questioning the authority of the Athenian leadership, but he was involved in fomenting rebellion against it. It was commonly believed that a number of his former students might have betrayed Athens for Sparta, eventually leading to the overthrow of the Athenian government.

Furthermore, his teaching of philosophical enquiry encouraged his students to question the merits and even the existence of divine powers. This was not a good time to choose, as the citizens of Athens assumed that their defeat had come about because their protective goddess Athena had punished them for not believing in her. Decimated by decades of war and with its empire much reduced around it, Athens had no time for the ramblings of a grumpy old man. To the vast majority of the public, his continued questioning of that which had made the Athenian Empire great had seemingly contributed towards its downfall.

The Socratic Method

Of course, this was not true. Socrates was openly critical of the Athenian establishment – and the way it conducted itself – as a result of encouraging his students to go back to first principles and question all established norms. More importantly, he demanded that his students challenge contemporary definitions of key moral concepts such as 'justice' and what should be considered 'good'. This was not to promote 'injustice' or 'evil' but to understand things better. His method of enquiry, later called the Socratic method, embraced a dialectic form in which answers to questions were a prelude to further questions, which ultimately induced diametrically opposed answers to the ones given in the first place. In a back-and-forth debate on the truth of widely held opinions, Socrates managed to make his conversational adversaries meet themselves coming the other way in arguments.

However, he was convinced that this methodology helped people get closer to their underlying beliefs and the extent of their knowledge. In particular, it unveiled the limitations of their knowledge. By its nature, therefore, the Socratic method is a negative method of hypothesis elimination: as people

11

steadily identify and eliminate those hypotheses that lead to contradiction, better and more resilient hypotheses emerge. During this process, the participants are invariably forced to examine their own belief systems – as well as their value systems – and where necessary revise them. As a result, a Socratic dialogue, once embarked on, becomes a rich and empowering form of conversation, leading to unexpectedly new and radical ideas.

It is highly unlikely that Socratic dialogue on its own posed a threat to the bitter remnants of the Athenian Empire. Nevertheless, it is undeniable that some of those who engaged in this form of dialogue became so adept at political debate that they could run rings around the unbending supporters of the status quo of the Athenian state. It is furthermore clear that, at a cruder level, the powers that be needed a scapegoat to answer for their downfall. "If you're not for us, you're against us", was their battle cry. All Socrates wanted was a better version of the truth. He wasn't so much a dissident as an asker of awkward and embarrassing questions. His reward for soliciting answers which were at variance with the official dogma was that damning description heard then, and now: enemy of the State.

And so it was that a public court found him guilty and he was sentenced to die by his own hand – a state-mandated suicide. He would ingest hemlock, a neurotoxin that disrupts the central nervous system. Death would be gradual as the poison crawled its way through the system, slowly robbing the extremities of the body of life and movement, turning it cold and rigid in its wake; and then eventually reaching the heart, insidiously crushing it, causing it to collapse.

It has often been asked why Socrates went to his death so peacefully; after all, he had other options, one being to escape. His followers had bribed the prison guards who were willing to assist in this regard. He could have then fled from Athens.

Yet instead he chose to drink hemlock knowing that it would kill him. His reasons, as he presented them to his followers, were, typically, philosophical in nature. He said that, as a citizen of Athens, he fully accepted that one should abide by its laws, even if they demanded an unjust punishment. Such an approach represented a 'contract' with the State. Should he break that contract he would harm society as a whole, something that was contrary to the Socratic code. He also said that true philosophers should not fear death, especially if in life they had achieved a measure of wisdom beyond their peers.

You have to hand it to Socrates for his conservative attitude towards the law and his acceptance of his fate. Given his disposition to argue the toss on everything, he must have harboured ambivalent feelings towards the people who had condemned him, and the fairness of his sentence. Yet he took it like a man – a remarkable man for any era and any generation. Fortunately for us, he passed on his methodology to Plato who laid it all out in his early works. And the torch still burns today, as you will see.

2 The Legendary Dialogue: Socrates & the Fox

Really, Ischomachus, I am disposed to ask: "Does teaching consist in putting questions?" Indeed, the secret of your system has just this instant dawned upon me. I seem to see the principle in which you put your questions. You lead me through the field of my own knowledge, and then by pointing out analogies to what I know, persuade me that I really know some things which hitherto, as I believed, I had no knowledge of.

SOCRATES, as quoted by Xenophon in *Oeconomicus* (The Economist) as translated by H G Dakyns.

Legend has it that shortly before his trial Socrates uncharacteristically left his students and followers and walked into some nearby woods on the outskirts of Athens. He wandered awhile before finding a place where the sun trickled through the trees and created a swathe of dappled light around a fallen, mossy log. He sat upon the log, closed his eyes and breathed deeply.

Completely isolated from human contact, he searched deep within himself with the intention of finding the true wisdom that had eluded him for so long. At the point when he almost lost complete consciousness of his surroundings, he became acutely aware that he was not alone. He glanced up to see that a fox was nearby, watching him. The filtered sun bathed the fox in an incandescent light, its fiery red coat seeming to shimmer and its white underbelly looking rich and silvery. Its amber eyes were fixed upon Socrates. It displayed no fear. The fox was clearly unperturbed by his presence; in fact it seemed more intrigued than worried. It slowly cocked its head to one side and stared intently at the quiet man before it.

Socrates' inquiring eye examined the creature in return. It was lean and hardy, its athletic form forged from a life of continual quest. Yet it also commanded the grace and poise of pampered nobility. Its angular features had been honed through constant searching and foraging. It had a cold and piercing hunter's eye, and yet its soft fur gave it a gentle and caring demeanour.

For a while they both looked at each other, each seeking a reason for the other's presence. Socrates sensed that the fox was asking him something. Was it possible, Socrates asked himself. He slowly shifted his weight, leaned slightly forward, extended both his open hands and in a polite but firm whisper, asked, "Does my presence concern you?"

The fox seemed to smile. "Perhaps I should ask," retorted the fox, "does my presence concern *you*?"

Socrates smiled back, gently shook his head and said, "Not at all." Indeed, he felt a deep and fulfilled calm wash over him in the presence of an intellect that obviously matched his. "I have been continually questioning anything and everything, hoping to find answers, and that's what finds me here," he added.

"I, too, search continually, and sometimes, in the process of meeting paradoxes and contradictions along the way, I find what I am looking for."

"Then," said Socrates, "knowing your reputation for quick-witted and agile thinking, you may be the one finally to help me". As Socrates looked at the fox to confirm the seriousness of his intent to engage him, the creature slowly cocked its head once more and met his gaze. At that moment they both realised that just as they had stumbled across each other, so had they found themselves. There was much to talk about. And so started a dialogue between Socrates and the fox.

The Dialogue

FOX: Most philosophers start by asking: "What is the meaning of existence?"

SOCRATES: I don't. For whatever species you are, how can you define the meaning or purpose of your existence unless you fully understand the context in which you exist?

FOX: You mean in my case understanding how the forest works. For instance, the relationships between the various animals inhabiting it and the impact they individually and collectively have on the environment.

SOCRATES: Yes, but also the impact that the environment has on them. For example, my present surroundings have created a deep sense of tranquillity in me. However, when I'm in the busy streets of Athens, the hustle and bustle excites me. A rule of existence is that wherever you go, and whatever people you encounter, you leave something behind and take something away with you. We are all elements of a system in a continual state of interaction and mutual influence, as our minds are with our bodies.

FOX: So I'm leaving a lasting impression on you with this conversation, as I know you are now doing on me?

SOCRATES: Correct. But to get back to your original comment, my first question is always: "Why are you what you presently are? What mixture of natural-born qualities and experiences since birth has made you into the animal, or in my case the person, you are today?" It's a question of fact, because we are dealing with the past. I am asking you to trace the single unique line between the moment you came into being till now. Think about all the influences on your life so far – positive, negative, neutral – which have conspired to get you to this location at this point in time.

FOX: That question would take longer to answer than I have time for, given the necessity for me to be constantly on the move in daylight hours. But, yes, I was born a fox with all the strengths and weaknesses that go with the species. My choice of parents was beyond my control, as was my date of birth. But what has been within my control since then has been to use my strengths instinctively to cover for my weaknesses. I am small and therefore vulnerable, but I am agile and have keen senses. I know my limitations, I know the risks, but I also grab opportunities as they arise. I can adapt to the changes in the environment, and, man, have there been some big changes recently! As far as I know, you're the first person to have ventured into this grove. You have to accept change, and change with it. Call it foxiness that keeps me alive, call it cunning intelligence, but here I am and my wife has kids on the way.

SOCRATES: I wish I could echo your upbeat approach. My destiny line has been different from yours. I was born into a fairly well-to-do family and had a conventional upbringing in Athens. As you rightly say, I had no choice but to be an Athenian which, to begin with, was the most marvellous thing to be, since Athens used to be the leading city on Earth. I got married and had three children, but then my world was turned upside down when my nation went to war with its neighbour, Sparta. I joined the army as an infantryman, or 'hoplite' as we call it, and served in several campaigns. Basically I went with the flow until I realised how futile the war was and how corrupt our society had become. Then I started asking questions and gathered a set of young followers around me with whom to debate these questions. I've never written anything down, but the questions I ask have got to the ears of the ruling authorities and have made them very angry. I am about to be put on trial and I feel a sense of impending doom. But then it was my choice. I was in control.

FOX: So is there anything you would change about yourself now? In that respect, you have wider choices than me because my occupation in the animal kingdom will forever remain the same. All I can do is move to another place.

SOCRATES: Don't be so humble, because that was going to be

my second question: No, I would never contemplate moving out of the field of philosophy or change where I live. But it is the question that logically follows the first one. Having traced your destiny line from start to present, where should you go to now? But then the third question has to be: "Who is for you, who is against you and who is neutral?" In seeking to clarify the direction you wish to take, you have to return to the principle of being part of an interconnected system.

FOX: So you have to weigh up your friends and enemies and those who can go either way before deciding on your next move? I like that, because in the animal kingdom you very quickly learn who is out to kill you and who isn't. You avoid the places where the former may be and stick to potentially friendly territory.

SOCRATES: With human beings it's more difficult to judge, for we have the quality of deceit. But nothing really happens unless you have a few or many people on your side and you find ways around those whom you have identified as obstructing you. This makes the fourth question easy to ask: "What are the rules of the animal kingdom and how do they differ from those governing human society?"

FOX: Well, I can only speak for my world. The rule is simple and all-encompassing: you do lunch, or be lunch. Straight competition. Survival of the fittest.

SOCRATES: In our world, that rule exists too in commerce and war. Nonetheless, I have spent all my philosophical hours on enquiring about another set of rules that should co-exist with the rule of competition. These relate to morality and goodness, but everybody has a different idea about what they are. I doubt whether we will ever reach agreement, but the quest must continue.

FOX: Having acknowledged that each of us in our own way is an element of a complex system, and that we should have knowledge of the other participants and the rules that apply to all of us, there is one more thing. Life can surprise you and it is better to be aware of the surprises in advance, or have a very fast reaction time if they really do come out of the blue. Don't you agree?

SOCRATES: Of course; and that leads me to my fifth question: "What are the uncertainties that can radically change your destiny line?" Because, make no mistake, the majority of factors making up the future environment around you are uncertain and beyond your control. What you are does not determine what you will be. In my case, I have no power over the court that is going to sit in judgment on my future, and I have to be prepared for all eventualities. On a broader front, the defeat by Sparta came as a big surprise to most Athenian citizens since they believed that they were the most advanced society in the world with the greatest military might. They have reacted badly because defeat was unthinkable. But there again, they might bounce back if defeat has taught them to be more 'foxy' about the future. Which naturally leads on to my next question, which is one of the hardest to answer: "Where is your destiny line going to lead you? What are the possibilities? What are the consequences?"

FOX: My possibilities are to take my wife and travel north, south, east or west after this conversation. Each path will contain its own string of events and consequences, which will become part of my destiny line. And you?

SOCRATES: That depends on the outcome of the trial. I could be found not guilty of any crime and continue to debate the issues that intrigue me. I could spend the rest of my life in prison. I could be put to death. Three scenarios for which there will be one outcome, but I must be prepared for all three. Now in light of the fact that you ought to move on soon, we need to get to the crux of the matter. What are we going to take away from our conversation and do? For as we both know, actions speak more loudly than words.

FOX: Ah! You are rushing ahead in the conversation. As I said earlier, my whole destiny line to date has involved a growing understanding of my strengths and weaknesses. So the seventh question should be: "What *are* your strengths and weaknesses and where are your immediate opportunities and threats?" Unless you tackle this question, talk of possible action is academic, with due apology to you as a philosopher. Yes, I agree that what you are does not automatically determine what you will be or what you *can* be, but it sure as hell has an influence over your next move.

SOCRATES: I told you at the outset that I thought you were smart. You are! Well, my strength is that I have an enquiring mind, and I guess my weakness is that I do not suffer fools gladly. My opportunity is to leave a legacy of the importance of not accepting things at face value; and the threat is imminent death.

FOX: Well put. Which neatly dovetails into my next – and if I've counted correctly the eighth – question: "What options do you have?" I've outlined mine, which are pretty simple and relate to the part of the forest I want to sleep in tonight.

SOCRATES: Hmm, I could escape before the trial starts and come along with you. But that would damage my legacy. I could reconsider my public stand on the war and the way Athens is governed, but that would also damage my legacy. I can stand trial and stick to my principles, in which event I've already laid out the future possibilities.

FOX: So now we come to your question: "Which option are you going to exercise and turn into action?" Personally I've decided to head north and take my chances there.

SOCRATES: This dialogue has been delightful because it has clarified my mind. Of course, I will exercise the last option and take my chances in court.

FOX: Well, dear friend, best of luck. It is time to part.

SOCRATES: Not before the final and tenth question. Remember, at the very beginning you thought that I was going to ask about the meaning of existence. Now we have discussed the past, the present and the future, we must return to this issue with the extra knowledge we have gained. "What for you is the meaning of life?"

FOX: I suppose it has to do with the reproduction of my species. That is my legacy. I have to protect my wife and children so that someday in some far distant country my several times great-grandchildren will carry on the foxy tradition.

SOCRATES: Yes, that is the meaning of life for me too. But I also want my idea of enquiry to persist in the minds of future generations.

FOX: In all probability, that will happen if you suffer the worst of all possible fates. Premature death will ensure eternal life for your idea.

SOCRATES: Your final remark, my dear friend, is – whether you intended it or not – a Socratic outcome. You are a 'seer' in the true meaning of the word. Not only do you see things more quickly than other animals because of your peripheral vision, you see things differently – stripped of the assumptions and 'laws' we all like to lay down. You see things as they really are and, by doing just that, you see into the future. My life's work has been trying to give people a fraction of your talent by asking questions that reveal the truth behind the mask of appearances. Goodbye and good luck.

With that they parted company, never to meet again, but never to forget the wisdom and experience they had shared with one another. Both had given and taken something away from the encounter. Both their destiny lines had intertwined and changed.

3 The Conversation Model: Our Version of the Socratic Method

*In every one of us there are two ruling and directing principles,
whose guidance we follow wherever they may lead; the one being
an innate desire of pleasure; the other, an acquired judgment which
aspires after excellence.*

SOCRATES, as quoted in Plato's *Phaedrus*

Little did the fox know when he responded to Socrates' question about the meaning of life that his wish to have several times great-grandchildren would be so spectacularly granted. For not only are there rural foxes in forests like his (but sadly even more encroached upon by man), his species are roaming around the streets of London, having adapted to living in an urban environment as well.

But the fox would have been even more amazed if he had been fast-forwarded to our den and met a pair of foxy, game-playing strategists who, in a small way, are the spiritual descendents of Socrates. We think that he would have totally approved of the methodology that we have designed to assist companies to have an effective strategic conversation about their future. It has a lot in common with the once-in-a-life-time conversation he had with Socrates in the sunny grove. He might have viewed it as a coincidence. But then he might have reflected that he did leave something behind in the chance encounter – something passed down through the generations.

The Evolution of the Model

From our side, we could have said to the fox that our methodology is unique and independently crafted. It has come about through rigorous application, re-evaluation and fine-tuning in the course of facilitating countless sessions in plenty of boardrooms. We've paid our dues. The claim is partially true, and we would like to thank all the CEOs and their teams who have voluntarily subjected themselves to our version of the Socratic method. However, we would have had to acknowledge to our furry friend that the seeds of our first book, *The Mind of a Fox – Scenario Planning in Action*, published in June 2001, lay in the foxy dialogue that took place 2 400 years previously. The matrix we introduced in the book was based on two key questions about the future which asked what is certain and uncertain about it, and what you control and don't control in it. These two questions, as you will remember, were posed in the conversation in the woods. Nevertheless, we do go further by suggesting that you will not get a proper idea of what you do control unless you start by delineating what you don't control. In other words, we really do believe in applying the type of hypothesis elimination, much loved by Socrates, to the formulation of strategy.

We have found that these two questions open up a whole new way of strategic thinking. Most people operate in a constrained frame of mind, boxed in by certainty and control. This is quite understandable, because it creates a level of constancy and sureness within which most people feel comfortable. When push becomes shove, we don't like change. Extrapolate that into the business environment and it will explain why many companies' strategic vision involves doing the same thing but better; or, to put it bluntly, staying in the same rut. It may explain why every company we work with finish off their strategic conversation enthusing about the depth and clarity of the insight they have gained. It's almost as if Socrates himself had had a hand in guiding the discourse away from the rut to higher ground. As the father of Western philosophy, he was a champion of venturing beyond the constraints of conventional wisdom. Perhaps he would have made an ideal nonexecutive director in today's boardroom.

We have been fortunate to work with a diverse portfolio of companies throughout the world, operating in fields such as banking, pharmaceuticals, mining, financial services and asset management, legal services, the media, retail, manufacturing and agriculture – from giant multinationals to family-run businesses. We've done stimulating sessions as well with municipalities, schools, universities, churches and NGOs. One of us has even conducted an 'informal conversation' at the Central Party School in Beijing. In each case, we noted any observations made by participants on how we could improve our methodology and adapted it accordingly. The result was a model for strategic conversation that was the subject of our second book: *Games Foxes Play – Planning for Extraordinary Times*, published in April 2005. Again a vein of Socratic dialogue ran through the book in that a methodology of questioning and self-examination was presented to help companies arrive at a more lucid understanding of their strategic choices. This was all done in the context of business being a game.

That vein of self-interrogation is now at the heart of this book. The strategic conversation model has again been evolved into a series of specific questions and sub-questions in order to effect a higher level, and more robust form, of strategic thinking, with due allowance for the complexity of the system that any organisation finds itself in. The secret lies in the nature of the dialogue that is encouraged, and how this is done. Socratic dialogue allows for in-depth understanding of issues through a combination of rigorous enquiry and developing consensus. Preferably performed in small groups, it enhances individual self-confidence while at the same time encouraging the common search for truth in a question-and-answer pattern. The dialogue allows participants to reflect and think independently and critically; but at the same time it engages them as a group to search for collective answers, not as an end in itself, but as a means of deepening the investigation of long-held paradigms and their validity. By combining the philosophy of Socratic dialogue and the model of strategic conversation we designed in our last book, we have arrived at a core list of ten questions that, we believe, provide true strategic wisdom if answered sincerely and fearlessly.

Bear in mind that it was the common quest for this penetrating type of wisdom that brought Socrates and the fox together in the first place; after all, what other animal embodies the perpetually enquiring mind of Socrates better than a fox? It is a noble creature that projects a demeanour and knowledge beyond its ranking in the kingdom of life. More importantly, for our purposes, the fox is the most apt metaphor to embody the character needed by companies to outwit their competitors and remain world class in today's rapidly changing business environment. In nature, the fox is quick-witted, adaptable and resourceful and has an astute awareness of its environment and the forces and relationships at play within it. Expressed in more philosophical terms, a fox thinks of life as a system comprised of many parts and inter-dependencies; and that it is only through the knowledge of the system as a whole that decisions can be optimised about the future. In terms of strategy, a fox will stick to a strategic path, but will regularly check the environment ahead to see if there are any changes that would require the strategy to be amended.

The fox knows that just as there are those elements of its environment that present themselves as food, so it is presented as food to others. If it interacts correctly with these elements it should survive. If it interacts successfully with these elements it will thrive. Because a fox is omnivorous and continually applies its inquiring instinct, it doesn't follow a rigidly predetermined course in the search for food. Neither is it limited to a particular type of food. The result is an animal that carries with it centuries of inbred experience about its environment, and which can thrive under virtually any circumstances. It has learnt a great deal about the nature of enquiring, the processing of the information that is gathered and the effective and speedy implementation of ideas. Imagine what insight such an animal could offer if it could talk, and especially with one of human history's most experienced and influential thinkers.

Games and Strategy

Hence, the relevance of our 'record' of the dialogue between Socrates and the fox. The dialogue's value should resonate further with modern business by the inclusion of the metaphor of a game in our second book (and which we repeat here). Games and business have a lot in common. Both are subject to rules. Both involve competing teams where the winner is usually the team with the greater skill and more effective strategy and tactics. Both contain inherent risks and uncertainties; and both have definite outcomes – you win, you lose, you draw: you make money, you go bust, you barely survive. Moreover, the outcome can turn on factors that are beyond the control of any individual player, factors that are often seemingly minor at the time they first manifest themselves. Think of the clouds on the horizon that eventually wash out a game of cricket.

However, there are also some very important differences between the game of business and games, say, of cards and sport. In the latter case the rules are agreed upon and never change during the course of play. Any changes to the rules are made in advance and with input from, and full acknowledgement of, the various stakeholders. In business, as in life, the rules rarely stay the same, and when they do change they can do so spectacularly, without notice and even to the point where the game becomes unplayable. The only rules that never change are the moral rules of the game (but even then, there are some people who will either disagree or openly bend or break these rules!). The game of business is far more complicated than any sporting game, and therefore demands a greater degree of imagination. Those who stick rigidly to an established strategy without incorporating the potential for changing rules will soon find themselves playing a different game to everyone else. Any seasoned business campaigner, operating within such a continually changing landscape, knows that strategy is more of an intuitive feel than a rational science. But both are required.

Thus business is not a game to be directed by planners who believe that the future is simply a projection of the past. Although we can study the past and learn from it, we can't plan for the future around the past. Neither can we accept that the future can be encapsulated into a single forecast on which you can bet the whole shop. No matter how expert the opinion you've obtained is, it can be utterly wrong. The future is always changing, evolving, and creating different, new challenges. Any opinion on it is automatically subjective. As Socrates so aptly remarked to the fox: "What you are does not determine what you will be." It makes sense then that before any decisions can be made around how to *play* the game, a strategic conversation should start with a robust *examination* of the game itself, and the swathe of possibilities accompanying it.

It is particularly apt that our concept of a strategic conversation should be inspired by the insight and wisdom of Socrates, because the word 'strategy' is Ancient Greek in origin, specifically derived from his home city of Athens. The term *strategos* referred to a commander in chief (or chief magistrate) who was a leading figure of authority in the Athenian democracy. A military *strategos* was expected to possess the ability to project and direct the larger military movements and operations of a campaign. In fact it is a term still used today in the modern Hellenic army to denote the highest officer rank. At some stage the term *strategos* was expanded to include the decisions made by such a person – and not just the person himself. For centuries, therefore, *strategos* or its English equivalent 'strategy' has been a term employed in the planning and conducting of warfare, specifically the movement of forces on the ground, the allocation of resources in support of those forces and the deception of the enemy.

Given the notoriously competitive and aggressive campaigns of leading corporate players, it was only a matter of time before the word 'strategy' became embraced by the world of business. Indeed, Sun Tzu's *The Art of War* – that famous Chinese military treatise that inspired centuries of great commanders including Napoleon, Mao Zedong and Douglas MacArthur, and even those behind Operation Desert Storm – is a popular addition to many boardroom libraries! For example, compare the quote of the famous Prussian General Karl von Clausewitz: "A good strategy is the successful preparation of a tactical victory" with Jack Welch's quote, "Strategy is the evolution of a central idea according to continuously changing circumstances." The CEO has become the general.

In its shift from the battlefield to the boardroom, 'strategy' has often been confused with 'tactics' and the two terms are sometimes used interchangeably, albeit erroneously. Perhaps it makes sense then that at this stage we spend a little time clarifying the difference between the two terms, especially with reference to their implementation in business. If we were asked to summarise the difference in one sentence, we'd say: 'strategy' is the direction of the business and 'tactics' are how to get there. To expand a little bit further we could borrow from an old nineteenth-century saying: "Strategy differs materially from tactics; the latter belonging only to the mechanical movement of bodies, set in motion by the former." What this means is that a handful of strategic decisions determine all future operational decisions. We therefore don't believe that the 24-point strategic plan recommended by some consultants is useful. Unless the overarching strategy is to go off in 24 different directions, the result can only be to sow confusion (which the consultants then have to resolve in their next contract!).

It is our belief that, through a proper strategic conversation, what should emerge are one or two simple and clear decisions around *direction*, and a prioritised list of actions, or tactics, on *how* to get there. It is important, especially in view of typical time constraints and resource limitations, that such a list of tactics should not be so exhaustive as to paralyse their overall implementation. Ask any manager about the dangers of analysis paralysis or any politician about the crisis of implementation. Hence the need to prioritise the tactics to extract maximum leverage. The latter forms an essential objective of any complete strategic conversation.

And who should develop a company's strategy? Someone from outside the company? Why bring in external consultants to dictate a company's strategic policy, knowing full well that once they have dished out their opinion and their words of wisdom, they will leave the company to its own devices? It makes sense that the best people to paint scenarios for a company and then shape that company's strategic direction should be those who are expected to implement that strategy. However, internal strategy sessions often follow a set format which runs the risk of perpetuating traditional stereotypes and conventional solutions. These sessions, therefore, have to be restructured in a way that jogs executives into a more robust analysis of the company and the changing environment in which it operates. By its very nature, Socratic dialogue does this. It transforms the spirit of the conversation from the normal, dreary type of superficial analysis that companies go through nowadays to a full-blooded, back-to-basics debate. It thereby creates a richer picture of the game, breaks all sorts of moulds along the way and produces nuggets of strategic wisdom from deep inside the most reticent minds around the table (which would otherwise never be discovered).

But how do you set such a dialogue in motion, and how do you keep it on track? The answer lies in the nature and structure of the questions. Presented correctly and in the right order, the questions change the conversation within a team, which then changes their minds, which then changes their behaviour and ultimately influences their actions. This is the causal sequence upon which our methodology is based. Interestingly, the nature of this questioning encourages further questioning within the team, in that some of the questions have no complete answers, but instead they demand that the team critically evaluates preconceived perceptions of the company and the business, or game, it is in. These invariably unearth contradictions between what the company is doing and what it should be doing. Bit by bit these contradictions are stripped away until a more accurate representation of the truth is achieved. This is the very foundation of the Socratic method of dialogue.

The Seven Principles

To change strategy you therefore need a highly inclusive conversation amongst people who can implement that change, where the process is based on ordinary but sound common sense. Nobody should lose the thread or be compelled to put their hand up and say: "Why ask that question now?" It all has to flow smoothly and logically. We base the sequence on seven straightforward principles pertaining to strategy:

1 Strategy is direction. Tactics are how to get there.
2 Strategy formulated without first consulting the context will probably end up being bad strategy.
3 Strategy is as much about ruling in potential paths that fit your scope as ruling out others that don't.
4 Good strategy can be turned into bad strategy by a future change in the context. Scenarios are a way of exploring alternative futures, which might necessitate a change in strategy.
5 Bad tactics can destroy good strategy, but no tactic can rescue bad strategy.
6 Good strategy has a greater chance of being converted into good results if tactics are accompanied by a set of measurable outcomes to which people can aspire.
7 Above all, strategy is about understanding what you do and don't control, and what is certain and uncertain about the future – and knowing when to change direction to avert unintended, and possibly tragic, consequences.

Principle 1 has already been explained. You have to aim the gun before you fire. Principle 2 is based on a quote by Lee Kwan Yew – the prime minister of Singapore between 1959 and 1990 – that those who don't learn from history are doomed to repeat it, and his insistence that he preferred to learn from history than through trial and error. Context is very important. In one session we facilitated, a comment was made that most countries only learn from their own mistakes and not from the mistakes made by other countries. So true when we look at history repeating itself around the world. Hence, in the questions we put, we want companies not only to learn from their own experience but from the experience of others as well. A pinch of trial and error can then be added as an extra ingredient!

Principle 3 is based on the fact that we all have specific

competencies and limited resources and therefore our playing field has to be clearly defined as to what activities lie inside (and are core) and what lie outside (and are non-core). Principle 4 says that we are all human and even the best-perceived strategy at the time can fail and therefore should be constantly road-tested by reviewing the environment and where it can go.

Principle 5 is so often broken because companies will simply not back new strategies with the level of resources required to make them succeed. The initiative is seen as 'nice to have' as opposed to being a crucial link in the company's evolution. On the flip side of no tactic rescuing bad strategy, think of going on holiday with the destination as strategy and getting there as a tactic. If the destination is bad, getting there quickly will only make the experience worse. Principle 6 explains why we all have budgets, goals, targets, objectives, key performance indicators and scorecards in business, because nothing gets done without measurement of progress.

Principle 7 is last but by no means least. It is a fact that people in power prefer to feel that they are in complete control, but our principle demands acknowledgement that they're not. They feel that they have exceptional foresight, but our principle asserts that the future is inherently uncertain and unpredictable. Worse still, many CEOs and politicians will simply not change their minds because they see it as a loss of face. Even when it is obvious that they should reconsider, they don't. Call it emotional unintelligence or myopia due to their personal make-up. Unpleasant facts will not be countenanced. This is in marked contrast to the philosophy put forward by the fox to Socrates when he said, "You have to accept change, and change with it."

Stubbornness, moreover, can lead to unintended consequences, where the law of tragic choices kicks in. This law says that you should take the least tragic choice to limit the amount of pain involved and perhaps open up other opportunities. What you can't do is nothing because no decent option immediately presents itself. Think of the choices Socrates had – tragic to say the least. But as the fox so rightly said: "Each path will contain its own string of events and consequences." Victory *can* be snatched from the jaws of defeat. If you live on the edge, you will always make mistakes. Learn to retrieve the situation instead of dwelling on failure.

The Ten Questions

These seven principles on strategy underpin our conversation model. We have now developed the model into a series of ten strategic questions through which we steer the participants. As can be seen in the table after the questions, 'defining the game' is really the strategic part of the discussion and 'playing the game' the tactics and outcomes you wish to achieve.

Defining the Game

1 **Context**: How has the game in your industry changed, where is it heading and how have you fared as a player?
2 **Scope**: What is your playing field today, and how do you want to expand (or contract) it in light of the developing context and the resources at your disposal?
3 **Players**: Who are the players that can most advance or retard your strategy, and how should you handle them in future?
4 **Rules**: What are the rules of the game that are likely to govern your strategy under all scenarios?
5 **Uncertainties**: What are the key uncertainties that could have a significant impact on the game and divert your course either positively or negatively?
6 **Scenarios**: On your gameboard, what are the possible sce-

narios and where would you position yourself in relation to them now?

Playing the Game

7 SWOT: What are your strengths and weaknesses as a player; and what are the opportunities and threats offered by the game?

8 **Options**: Within your span of control, what options do you have to improve your current performance and longer-term prospects in the game?

9 **Decisions**: Which options do you want to turn into decisions right now, and what is the initial action associated with each decision?

10 **Outcomes**: What is your meaning of winning the game in five years' time, expressed as a set of measurable outcomes?

The sequence of the questions can be explained in the following framework:

Question	Frame of Reference
1	Context
2	Strategy
3, 4, 5, 6	Testing the robustness of the strategy
7, 8, 9	Tactics, decisions, actions
10	Measurable outcomes

Straightforward though the questions may seem, they have multiple layers to them because they explore both the game as well as the player's relationship to the game. There are sub-questions as well. As Socrates said to the fox: "We are all

34

elements of a system in a continual state of interaction and mutual influence, as our minds are with our bodies." To reflect this philosophy, the course of the strategic conversation continually weaves between internal questions about the organisation and external questions about the environment, the relationship between the two often evolving as the conversation progresses. Moreover, please don't treat the frame of reference as a list to which strict adherence has to be given. At any stage, an issue may be raised that demands that you revisit an earlier stage of the conversation. Or a bright idea comes up before its time. Brilliance is spontaneous, not ordered! So look at our ten questions as segments of a circle which can be rotated clockwise or anticlockwise as circumstances require.

Those familiar with business strategy will realise that the roots of our model and our thinking lie in scenario planning. What we have done through our ten questions is to integrate scenario planning into the mainstream process of strategic planning and decision-making. It allows top executive teams of companies to test the resilience of their strategies and tactics against alternative scenarios and, should the need arise, come up with other options faster and more effectively than their competitors.

And how successful is the model? Pierre Wack was the recognised master of scenario planning during the 1970s and 1980s. He used to say that the acid test for any successful scenario exercise was not that it captured an unusual future before it happened; rather it was whether the scenario penetrated the mindset of the relevant decision-makers and persuaded them to act ahead of time. We call this the 'Wack test'. The scenario itself did not have to be entirely accurate in its details, as long as, in retrospect, it modified for the better the course of action taken.

Many scenario exercises are brilliant intellectually, but fail the Wack test because they do not connect to the people who make the decisions. There are, however, three aspects to our conversation model which give the scenarios a good chance of passing the Wack test:

- We assist the decision-makers in writing the scenarios themselves instead of having external specialists presenting scenarios to them. The decision-makers are an intrinsic part of the scenario process;
- We have integrated options, decisions and measurable outcomes into the same conversation that handles the formulation of the scenarios. Thus the practical implications of the scenarios cannot be ignored; and,
- The scenarios sometimes feature the main decision-makers in the story. This makes them feel more committed to take appropriate action to ensure greater probability of the virtuous scenario materialising, and the worst-case scenario being avoided.

Of course our conversation can still fail the Wack test. If it does, it is often through the sheer inertia – or the resistance to change – of the team. This invariably brings about a crisis in implementation and a reversion back to old and defective ways that are out of sync with the new game. Equally, inertia can also be experienced when no effort is made to cascade the strategy through the ranks, and make effective use of all the players in a team. CEOs love to talk about motivating their players but often don't provide a clear direction. They rule by the mushroom method – keep the staff in the dark and occasionally pour manure over them. Never mind passing the Wack test, these CEOs need a whack!

Such inertia is one of the aspects that we address when we facilitate strategic sessions using our conversation model. We deal with this challenge towards the end of the dialogue by breaking actions down into easily manageable deliverables, and making very pointed notes of who is going to do what by when. It is then up to the team to monitor progress.

The Mechanics

Looking more generally at how we implement the model, we predominantly work with a company's top executive team but, at times, with middle management. Sometimes we take on individual divisions or business units. We have also worked with organisations that have multiple stakeholders from diverse backgrounds – where common ground needs to be achieved before any plan of action can be put in place. A shared perception of the game helps enormously in these circumstances.

The choice of venue for any session is important. We do not advise using a company's office premises, as it is far too easy to suffer temporary loss of participants during the conversation. There are few things more frustrating than people nipping in and out to return calls or deal with day-to-day business. On the other side of the coin, resorts that offer an exciting array of activities, especially golf, can prove just as much of a distraction. We insist in these instances on work, *then* play, so the conversation is not overly disrupted.

The venue also requires careful thought because conversation often continues outside the room out of official working hours. We recommend a venue that matches the culture of the company. We once held a session in a wine cellar that was arranged (not by us, we must add) for a company renowned for their maverick, expressive persona. We all found it quaint, but incredibly restrictive and claustrophobic. One of the most exotic venues was the main cabin of a paddle boat. As it forged down the river, you could not help feeling that it epitomised the calm and resolute manner in which the company was being guided into the future.

Strategic conversations with multinationals carry with them extra challenges, not least around logistics and different languages and cultures. A little more patience and sensitivity is all that is sometimes necessary. We once facilitated, using video-conferencing, a session on sustainable development with a leading multinational company that was spread over a number of countries. Although, with the digital delay, the session was a little more challenging, it was softened by the knowledge that we had produced fewer carbon emissions by not flying delegates to a single destination!

When planning a strategic session with a company, we suggest a venue that allows the executive team, or participants, to sit at a round table or in a horseshoe configuration so they can see each other. Socrates did this with his pupils. Conversation is as much about gestures and facial expressions as it is about what people actually say. A behavioural psychologist once said that if you see someone looking upwards to the left, he or she is about to tell you a huge lie! Sitting in a circle also means that nobody has superior status at the table because of position. It's important to create an environment that encourages the conversation to be as participative as possible, since the best strategists in a team are often the last people who want to speak up. Foresight is very different from charisma.

We also insist on zero paper except, if necessary, a flip chart upon which we record the conversation. Preferably, though, we like to capture the proceedings on a screen linked to a computer where we can move back and forth on points made. We want people to bring their minds, their experiences and, most of all, their imagination, to the meeting. Long documents on strategy tend to contain figures that are based on consensus forecasts and therefore kill the imagination, the very faculty that allows people to think outside of the box. Such documents also seek alignment before the conversation has taken place, when the whole point of the conversation is to obtain a diversity of views and then gain alignment. Above all, long papers on strategy normally confuse strategy with tactics.

In terms of the number of participants, this depends on what the session is trying to achieve. If the session is designed to develop a new strategy and identify a company's strategic advantage over its competitors, confidentiality is paramount. So it makes sense that the group is limited to the executive team and/or the most senior management. We have even facilitated a conversation with one person – this amounted to executive coaching. If a session is designed to promote buy-in across various levels within a company and to ensure inclusiveness of the conversation, then a larger group would make sense. However, too large a group runs the risk of becoming like a conference plenary session and destroying the intensity of the conversation. Our experience has shown that the optimal number is between 5 and 20 persons, with a maximum of 25; anything larger than that and the spontaneity of the conversation could be lost.

Should, however, for reasons of inclusiveness, the number of persons exceed 25, they can be divided into smaller groups, with the conversation being held within those groups. But a caution must be given. We do believe that our conversation model is holistic and cannot be broken down into parts, with each group, say, doing a different set of questions (such as one group working only through questions 1-6 and another questions 7-10). Hence, in such a case, we prefer each group to work through the entire conversation model and then report back to the rest of the groups, after which a synthesis can be done of the data. This allows the thinking to be subjected to the rigours of the ten questions while at the same time providing a diversity of perspectives and insights. Furthermore, it can also give an indication of whether the thinking and understanding of the business or game has some commonality across the diverse groups, or whether each group perceives the game differently. Breaking into smaller groups can work when discussing options, as long as everybody has participated in the section on strategy and scenarios, and contributed towards the SWOT analysis.

The next question we are often asked is: how long does a typical strategic conversation take? Well, how long is a typical piece of string? Some conversations are highly interactive and explore wide areas around the business or game, whereas others are intense, to the point and characterised by a high degree of agreement. The number of participants can also influence the duration of a strategic conversation, as can the logistics required for group work. Realistically though, a good strategic conversation should take not less than a day and, being sensitive to the time constraints of a typical world-class company, should take no longer than two days.

A post-workshop write-up is invaluable to the process as it provides an ongoing working document through which the conversation can continue. It also provides a frame of reference to look back on when participating in future conversations. The write-up can be done by the facilitator once all the data has been collected and assimilated; or someone within the group can process the data during the conversation and then disseminate it amongst the participants immediately afterwards, either by e-mail or internal post. However, during all workshops, data must be captured and displayed visually to the participants as a constant record of the conversation.

Two other practical questions we are often asked about the model are:

- How often should you conduct these strategic conversations?
- How far down the organisation should you go with these conversations?

The answer to both questions is that there is no set formula, and it is very much up to each person or company as to how to use our model. Some people like to have a one-off conversation on strategy and then only review it if and when the external environment changes to the point that it has to be reviewed. Obviously, any tactical decisions taken at the meeting along with their associated actions are regularly monitored. Certainly the scenario gameboard is reviewed at appropriate intervals to keep the team aware of its competitive position and possible changes to the environment. Other teams like to have a strategic conversation once a year before the next round of operational planning and budgeting begins. This is fine as long as it doesn't become a bureaucratic chore.

On the second question, some companies like to restrict the conversation to their top executive team, while others like to cascade it down through the different business units and service departments. Obviously, the lower one goes, the more restricted the scope of the game becomes. Nevertheless, it is still useful to consider the range of activities inside any production unit/service centre and whether these should be changed to accommodate the needs of other in-house departments, which are its clients. Equally, relationships with 'supplier' departments can be examined as well.

One company we worked with first held a strategic conversation amongst its executive team. Then each member of the team facilitated the conversation further with his or her region or department. We were not involved in the second step except as bystanders. Such a process developed the conversation into an important internal communication tool; and allowed the conversation to become a feedback mechanism to the executive. The whole company was thereby strategically empowered since all employees and management shared a common understanding of the game and the direction in which the organisation intended to go.

A word or two on the attributes of a good facilitator:

- It should always be borne in mind that the correct strategic combination to take a company forward is invariably within the minds and experience of the participants. It is simply the role of the facilitator to help the participants identify it. Therefore a good facilitator coaxes brilliance out of participants, rather than comes up with brilliant ideas himself or herself. Hence, the role of the facilitator is different from the role of a consultant.
- The facilitator should not be overly knowledgeable about the nature of the company's business. It sounds surprising, but there is a good reason for this. In helping the facilitator to familiarise himself or herself with the nature of the company's business, the participants are often forced to return to basics and examine the game from a fresh perspective – unlike anything they have done for years. Having said that, a facilitator should not go into a session completely ignorant of the game under debate since valuable time will be wasted.

Those with a knowledge of philosophy will find a resonance in the above two attributes with the founding principles of Socratic dialogue. In the dialogue between Socrates and the fox, each of them played a role as a facilitator in the conversation, just as they did that of participant and listener. The result was a conversation that flowed freely, where preconceived ideas were tested and where the participants felt sufficiently liberated to review their strategy.

The remaining chapters will take you through the ten strategic questions in more detail. A flexible set of sub-questions will be developed and examples provided to illustrate the relevance of these questions. The final chapter is the conclusion of our strategic conversation with you and a tribute to Pierre Wack.

But before you take the next step, we think it's necessary that you understand the impact it might have: our experience has shown that once people have been introduced to this methodology, the quality of their enquiry and the level of thinking about their future are permanently elevated to a new level. This will have an overall beneficial effect on your company's level of strategic skills, thereby reducing (or removing) the reliance on the opinions of external consultants and the regular transfusions of wisdom they try to inject into your corporate bloodstream. With our questions, we extract the innate wisdom residing in the minds of the executives around the table. We all learn at the same time – like Socrates did in his dialogues with his students, mutually exploring issues and mutually resolving them in the give-and-take of debate.

Furthermore, we give the executive team the 'quality of sight'. In today's age, where perception is often regarded as reality and spin merchants abound to provide convincing and sometimes contagious perceptions, seeing through the veil – or the 'mask of appearances' as Socrates described it – is vital to success. Whether you are looking at yourself or the world around you, the hype has to be filtered out to make good decisions about the future. You need X-ray vision!

Some comments made as a result of our sessions are:

It was a turning-point because we used the positive scenario derived from the conversation to establish a new set of values and practices throughout the organisation – all the way down to grassroots level. CEO, BANKING GROUP

Normally I start a meeting by asking what the takeaways are likely to be. I note that, instead of answers, the takeaway will be some questions on strategy to keep me awake at night. I guess that's what Socrates had in mind. CEO, NATIONAL BAKERY CHAIN

43

As a small business, we are too busy doing business to take time out to think about the future. Nor can we afford to have a full-time strategic planner. So the conversation was an ideal way to take stock of our game briefly and passionately. Did you notice there wasn't a single interruption from a mobile phone? That has to be a first!

CEO, ATM SERVICE PROVIDER

We are all fierce individualists in our family. For the first time, we've had a conversation about the business which has brought us together as a team. No doubt in a few weeks time we'll be going our separate ways again, but at least we'll have the minutes of this meeting as proof of a fleeting moment of unity.

CHAIRMAN, FAMILY FOOTWEAR BUSINESS

I'm looking at my watch. You said five hours for the conversation and we've done it. Unbelievable!

CEO, MINING CONTRACTOR

I like the game analogy because it will give us a better way to process information in the future. If there's a new player, a new rule of the game or the emergence of a new market scenario, we will be able to adjust faster than our competitors. That's the name of the game.

DIRECTOR, ASSET-MANAGEMENT COMPANY

What is nice about your model is that it doesn't get in the way of discussing the business. It's invisible because it's so logical. I much prefer it to those methods with cheesy names where you spend half the time figuring out your next step.

CHAIRMAN, TIMBER COMPANY

I came in feeling paper withdrawal symptoms, but you've cured me of the habit. In future, I shall consign all thick strategy documents to File 13. I hope it doesn't get me into hot water!

EXECUTIVE, MUNICIPAL WATER BOARD

DEFINING THE GAME

4 Context: How has the game in your industry changed, where is it heading and how have you fared as a player?

The unexamined life is not worth living.
SOCRATES, as quoted in Plato's *Apology*

Every organisation has a destiny line that can be drawn from its genesis through its current form and into the future. The line is jointly determined by two factors: the internal development of the organisation as expressed in its actions and results and the external evolution of the environment in which it is operating. "For every action, there is a reaction," said Sir Isaac Newton a few centuries ago in laying down a universal law of nature. Ironically there is no better example of this than in the relationship between man and nature. Each leaves its indelible mark on the other. The African philosophy of *ubuntu* expresses the idea perfectly: "I am because you are." Yet strategy sessions give scant attention to this fact. The organisation is treated almost as an island unto itself. Few of its surroundings are taken into account in plotting the next move. So we start with an in-your-face question that emphasises the historic and future interrelatedness between the industry (or whatever you like to call your immediate environment) and you.

Socrates talks about his 'destiny line' in his dialogue with the fox and in so doing gives context to his life. Our first question is all about context, for the very good reason that no strategy can be appropriate unless it is contextually valid. A strategy to hike northwards on the gently rolling green hills of England in ordinary gear is contextually valid, and therefore passes muster. On the other hand, a strategy to hike northwards through the Arctic waste to the North Pole in the same clothes is not appropriate, unless the objective is to satisfy the cravings of a foolish, extreme, adrenalin-driven junkie!

The opening question may seem simple on the surface, yet the insight from it sets the scene for the rest of the conversation. We need to know where we have come from before we can decide where we want to go; and we need to know what is going on around us at the moment. In brief, we need to understand the present state of the game as well as its history and where it seems to be moving into the future. We used to call this 'painting a rich picture' of the system you inhabited. But the question serves other purposes as well. It is a comfortable way to initiate the strategic conversation, to warm people up for the more difficult questions ahead. It explores familiar territory and coaxes the participants into presenting their interpretations of the past before venturing their opinions on the future. It makes them painfully aware that the vast majority of the changes that have happened in the game are beyond their control. It helps shift their mental models to the point that they begin to think like foxes about adapting their strategies to current realities. Indeed, the neutrality of the opening question precludes any attempt by individuals to be defensive about their previously stated positions. Instead, it provides a departure point for a new alignment on which the future of the business can be built.

The Viability of the Game

Once the question has been presented and answered, the extent of the changes to the game become significantly, and sometimes frighteningly, explicit. Often one of the first things that emerges is how many drivers of change there are. These may include technology, consumer taste, consolidation of customers or opposition players, the weather, political shifts, legislation, and the emergence of countries like China and India as serious contenders in the global arena. Sometimes there may be only one or two main drivers, but often there are many, and by grouping or clustering them it is possible to get a better picture of their impact on the game. Some games may be undergoing such a transformation that the initial decision may be that it's best to exit the game and try another one altogether.

This type of conclusion may emerge through reflecting on the last part of the question: ". . . how have you fared as a player?" It invites an examination of whether you have simply survived and kept up with the game or been in a position to influence the present outcome to your advantage – in which case you may be in the winning circle. If neither of these views resonates with you, then the best decision may indeed be to switch games; in which case the tone has been set for the rest of the strategic conversation. In judging your performance, though, a critical feature is whether you have merely responded passively to all the changes in the game or actually initiated some of them yourself. Obviously, it makes a big difference to your status as a player if you are a trendsetter as opposed to a 'dedicated follower of fashion'.

Often companies don't have a good understanding of their positioning in the game and survive from day to day on intuition. Some of the world's greatest leaders were blessed with intuition, and often had more than their fair share of luck. But intuition is a fickle companion, and if it lets you down it can do so disastrously and with a debilitating effect on your self-confidence and the confidence others have in you as a leader. Much better to have a healthy bout of introspection with your team and objectively consider your collective performance to date. Obviously, if a critical examination of the game shows that you are winning, the strategy going forward is not about enjoying the ride; it's about consolidating and enhancing your position. However, if you are in the losers' corner then the conversation will be more about changing strategic direction or, as mentioned earlier, changing games completely. Don't underestimate how hard it is to get a company to admit to being in the second situation. Once, it had to take a halving of the company's share price in the six months following the workshop to get the message through to management that fundamental change was essential.

When some businesses have examined the game and seen how they are faring, they feel a little concerned about their size in relation to other, larger players, as well as their measure of influence over the game that may be developing in complexity. This is important to note, but not a point to worry about. Smaller companies are often more agile than larger companies; they can change or adapt more easily, and they can manoeuvre around the gameboard more quickly. Size doesn't always matter; what *is* crucial in the game, though, is *momentum*. In physics, this is the product of a body's mass and velocity; so a larger company that is slow to innovate can have less momentum in the game than a smaller company that is continually hastening forward in accordance with the changes in the game. And the games of business are *always* changing.

It is the extent and speed of changes within a game that define its attractiveness or otherwise. Massive changes will contribute to the game's volatility and unpredictability. These can swallow up the most hardened players – whether they are large or small. Those remaining have to move into uncharted territory as they battle to reconfigure their game plan to deal with the changes. The answers to this first question in the strategic conversation bring such changes to the fore and demand that participants reflect on whether they are up to the challenge with their existing capabilities and experience, or need to start anew as pathfinders in a 'brave new world'.

Working with multinationals has its own special challenges. We have seen many such companies take a deep breath when the full scale of the game they are in is revealed to them. In the majority of cases their game is more a set of smaller games running concurrently. In some of them they may be a larger player with a dominant market share, and in some they may be a new, smaller player in the process of establishing their credentials. Each game has its own set of drivers for change.

But as a multinational, you have to take cognisance of how the global geopolitical game has changed as well; and perhaps how the game is changing in each of the countries where you are doing business. Ian Fleming in his book *From Russia with Love* made the best case we've seen for looking at the bigger picture. Imagine you're playing billiards, and the ball you've just hit is going into the pocket because you have obeyed the laws of the billiard table. However, a pilot in a jet above you faints at the controls, the plane crashes into the building and the building collapses on you and the table. The ball misses the pocket! End of story – even if you are James Bond. The big picture wins.

Finally, when presenting this first question in a strategic conversation, we've often heard that business follows set cycles and that "not to worry, things will pick up, they always do". If this is the case and these cycles are predetermined, why is it so few companies survive more than a few cycles? Resilient companies critically examine the nature of the ebbs and flows in the game and distinguish between the cyclical patterns and the changes that are permanent. They adjust to the latter.

Here are some examples of insights that have come to light in response to the first question of our strategic dialogue. They constitute preparation for the tough questions ahead:

The game changed in 1978 when Deng Xiaoping became leader and introduced the open- door policy. China's economy at the time was ranked around 100th in the world and now it is number 4. Not bad to rise 96 places in 28 years. We'll soon overtake Germany to be number 3. I wonder when the West will stop calling us an emerging economy!   CHINESE STRATEGIST, BEIJING

Thanks for the opening question. It has given me an unbiased perspective of my business. And, as the Irish would say, to get from A to B, you must start by knowing exactly where A is.
FAMILY BUSINESS OWNER

A few years ago, we had teenagers in the shops buying CDs. *Now they download music off the internet onto iPods and the only customers we get are people in their 40s and older who can't. It's a middle-aged game now, so maybe we should only stock adult contemporary and gospel.*   EXECUTIVE, MUSIC RETAIL CHAIN

Mining in the last century was a dull game of constant surpluses, where the company that won was the company that could cut its costs faster than its competitors. Now, none of us can keep up with Chinese demand, so we're all scrambling for resources; and the guy who wins will be the guy with the smartest geologists or the best relationship with the exploration juniors who discover big new deposits.   MANAGER, MINING MULTINATIONAL

Radio once was a 'lean forward' game where people listened to their favourite serials at any time of the day or night. Now it's a 'sit back' game with two peaks at morning and afternoon rush hours and relaxation stuff in between.   CEO, BROADCASTING GROUP

For the last 25 years, we've had below average rainfall and an increasing population. 2006 was the 'big dry' – an absolute stinker for rain. We're constructing a desalination plant, but you feel there's

been a structural shift in the game to the point where environmental constraints are going to dictate the outcome.

MUNICIPAL CEO, PERTH, AUSTRALIA

MBA *programmes were for a long time the money-spinners for business schools and they're still seen as the flagship course by which status is judged. But advanced management programmes and short-term executive courses tailored for individual companies are where the real money lies nowadays.*

DEPUTY DEAN, LEADING BUSINESS SCHOOL, USA

We used to have a Government Board selling our product. But it was abolished just when our customers – the retailers – were consolidating into larger groups. How have we fared? Terribly, because we're price takers with no negotiating clout and a falling percentage of the value chain. The game has become so unplayable that the definition of child abuse in agriculture is handing on your farm to your son.

SOUTH AFRICAN FARMER

My grandfather was a tailor in Munich in the early 1930s and ran an extremely profitable business. But when he saw Hitler changing the game, he decided to emigrate to America. If he hadn't read the signs and seen the possibilities, I probably wouldn't be around for this conversation.

JEWISH PROPERTY DEVELOPER

The British game has changed dramatically. We once mined coal, forged steel and built ships and cars. We were an industrial nation. Now, the Chinese have captured the manufacturing space and the British have had to adjust by moving into other spaces the Chinese can't yet replicate – like financial services. But judging by the performance of the economy and the low level of unemployment, we've done it rather well.

INDUSTRIALIST, WOLVERHAMPTON, ENGLAND

5 Scope: What is your playing field today, and how do you want to expand (or contract) it in light of the developing context and the resources at your disposal?

The nearest way to glory is to strive
to be what you wish to be thought to be.
SOCRATES

After answering the first question, you should be beginning to see your business as it really is. No blinkers on. When Socrates commended the fox at the end of the conversation, he said: "You see things as they really are and, just by doing that, you see into the future."

Now we're not about to turn you, the readers, into a bunch of professional 'seers', but it makes absolute sense for you to have no illusions about the game you're in and the shape of your business before you decide what you are going to do next. In other words, once you have judged the worth of your game and your current ability to play in it, you can move on to define your scope – namely the specific area within which you want to be a player in the future.

Inwards and Outwards

Nevertheless, we stress that, life being a continuum, you must consider it as a destiny line. Remember Socrates' question to the fox: "Having traced your destiny line from start to present, where should you go to now?" Of course, many individuals lead incredibly varied lives, starting out as soldiers and becoming pop singers (James Blunt) or moving on from selling avant-garde vinyl records to becoming the most famous British entrepreneur in modern times (Sir Richard Branson). You can do that as an individual because you don't carry the responsibilities that a company does. In the latter case, before you do anything radical, you have to face up to the looking glass and consider some – if not all – of the following: the expectations of your employees and shareholders, your culture, your core competencies, your organisational structure, your business model, the resources at your disposal, your location, your public reputation and brand, etc.

Succinctly, your DNA or corporate make-up – the glue that holds you together – plays a role in determining your future destiny line.

Sure, you can decide that the present game is unplayable and strike off in an entirely new direction. But, like the fox who admitted his options were limited to the four principal points of the compass, there are restrictions placed on organisations beyond a certain size. They're like supertankers that need plenty of space and time to turn. Yet again, when looking at future scope, you have to look inwards and outwards at the same time.

Moreover, defining a playing field isn't simply a case of plotting the addresses of your factories or your customers on a map. Business, unlike sport, does not have the clearly drawn lines of a football field or a tennis court. You can decide on your own boundaries, subject to the limitations we have just mentioned. But there *have* to be lines you don't cross, because focus is a key element of a successful strategy. Hence, it is important to define your current playing field upfront, and decide what you want it to be in the future. For this reason we have made 'scope' our second question after 'context'. It is a purely strategic question because it defines the direction in which you wish to go and towards which all the internal players in your business should be aligned. Once the scope has been agreed on, it is possible to start positioning your players, motivating their actions and rewarding their performance as individuals and as a team.

You may remember the fox describing his destiny line thus: "I was born a fox with all the strengths and weaknesses that go with the species. My choice of parents was beyond my control, as was my date of birth. But what has been within my control since then has been to use my strengths instinctively to cover for my weaknesses. I am small and therefore vulnerable, but I am agile and have keen senses. I know my limitations, I know the risks, but I also grab opportunities as they arise".

The fox makes an important point: understand what you can and cannot control and define your playing field accordingly. This is not a formula to be unambitious. You'd most probably be surprised at the potential scope of your playing field once you have acquired a genuine knowledge of yourself as a player. In this respect, the fox underlines another important factor: play to your strengths and employ them wherever possible to make up for your weaknesses. Nobody is superhuman, no company is perfect. People or companies that feel they are flawless or omnipotent lose the plot immediately. Sound business strategies juxtapose your capabilities with the requirements of the game. This does not mean that new capabilities cannot be built; it simply underlines the importance of having a proper understanding of what those new capabilities are and putting sufficient resources into developing them. Think back to school and the sports you chose (apart from those which were compulsory!). It was all about constantly matching your skills to the games chosen. 'Constantly' is a crucial word here, because strategy and tactics are dynamic, particularly in grudge matches with the competition. The side that innovates and adapts its game is usually the one that comes out on top. Thus, it's the ability to change your mind and transform yourself – as a person or as a team – that keeps you in the forefront of the game. Champions never stand still.

Nations and Cities

This concept is as applicable to countries and companies as it is to schools. Let's start with countries. The global playing field of the last century was divided up into segments, marked off from one another by barriers of language, culture and politics. A few, well-entrenched major-league players such as Western Europe, the US and, latterly, Japan, dominated the central field, occasionally teaming up with smaller players who came on as substitutes but who otherwise remained on the sidelines playing their own games. Some never came on at all, although continually in an expectant state of warm-up; they just couldn't make the grade into the main game. Others, meanwhile, chose to do their own thing on an isolated field with no intention of ever joining in.

Globalisation has changed all that. The field is flatter, the barriers to entry lower, the relationships between the players more interdependent. We still have losers (failed states), but significant new players have emerged who have their own ideas on how the game should be played. They've thrown out the old rulebooks, thus forcing a serious rethink on the part of the previously reigning champions: how can we be congruent with the new conditions and maintain our competitive edge? Well, like everybody else, they have to play to their strengths and develop new ones out of their old ones at the same time. The scope of their economies and their exports should reflect this, as David Ricardo (an English economist) first observed in his *Principles of Political Economy* published in 1817. His celebrated principle of comparative advantage stated that countries would most benefit by specialising in goods that they produced efficiently and trading these for other goods produced more efficiently by other countries. Ricardo was a foxy economist!

As we all know, China is dominating large chunks of the

manufacturing game, using its vast resources of cheap labour to make the 'China price' its key differentiator. Russia, Africa and South America are principal players in the resources game along with the Middle East, which has been there a long time. The West has moved on to the hi-tech and services sectors, while everybody plays some role in the agricultural and tourist games. Each country has come up with a scope or product offering that suits its natural advantages, whether it be minerals, climate, diversity of fauna and flora, spectacular features of nature, etc., as well as the skills of its citizens (which may have been acquired over generations). Moreover, a nation's economic focus changes over time. For example, the UK has progressed from agriculture through manufacturing to services but retains elements of all three.

What is true for nations is also true for cities and towns. Each city/town has its own character and location conferring certain advantages on it. Nevertheless, the really successful ones rejuvenate themselves with new industries, layouts and centres as they change with the times. Think of Glasgow and Barcelona and how their scope expanded to include culture and the arts, or new cities like Dubai which has established itself as an entrepôt in the Middle East.

Companies, Schools and NGOs

So, back to business. What type of sub-questions do we ask to define scope? Interestingly, we have found that the list applies equally to organisations of noncommercial kinds ranging from NGOs to schools to universities to municipalities and even churches. The principal sub-question is: what lies at the centre of the field, on the margin and outside its boundaries? That is, what is the absolute core of your business, what is the outer core that adds value to the inner core and what is non-core? Obviously non-core operations can be phased out or disposed of; or if the service is still required it can be contracted out.

A multinational estate agency we worked with provided a good example of the application of this sub-question. The core activity is selling houses. However, linked to this are other activities that may add value to the transaction, such as furniture removal and relocation and satisfying other lifestyle requirements associated with purchasing a new home. These are not core to the business, but they do add value. The more elements you have in your product line by cross-selling or acting as a one-stop shop, the more value you add to the business and the better your game. Where the estate agency lacked the competence to deliver the extra service, they outsourced the activity.

The second subsidiary question is: should the field be wider or more focused? One truck and bus manufacturing group we worked with offered 132 different models of trucks and buses, of which only eight were regular sellers. Basic business logic suggested the playing field needed to be more focused. Generally speaking, it became no longer fashionable during the 1990s to be a conglomerate. Hence the decade saw the dismantling of conglomerates with a greater emphasis on smaller playing fields where competencies were historically strong. One group sold off a bank, an insurance company, a property company and a whole range of industrial interests in order to revert to its traditional business of mining.

The converse must also be addressed by examining the scope in order to extend the field into new, profitable activities. Many supermarkets, clothing and lifestyle retailers now sell cellular services, handsets and airtime, something that used to be the sole concern of cellphone retailers. This represents the embracing of a whole new, and highly profitable, business for these retailers. At the same time cellular networks enjoy significantly higher sales because the retailers have the capability to reach consumers *en masse* – something that isn't a core competency of the cellular networks. Nevertheless, there is a major difference between the strategy of the old rootless conglomerates and what is now going on. Today, you expand into 'adjacent areas' where your competencies can be stretched or incrementally adjusted to make you a serious player in the new game. The only old-style conglomerate businesses left these days are family businesses run by founders with the Midas touch (and General Electric!). It requires a very special talent to play several games simultaneously where the culture and skills for each one are very different. Imagine alternating hands of bridge with hands of poker.

To achieve more clarity in the debate on scope, we divide the playing field into product range, product chain, market segment and geographical footprint.

Product Range

This comprises the *horizontal* range of goods and services offered by your company. In other contexts, it would be the curriculum and extracurricular activities of a school, the number of faculties at a university or the range of services undertaken by an NGO. Questions around your product range should include:

- Is there something new you should add?
- Is there something you should delete either because it is non-core or because it is consuming too many of your resources?
- Do you have something unusual in your product/service line-up which differentiates you from your competitors? If not, shouldn't you?
- Is your product mix correct or should it be shifted in line with changes in the demands of the market?

This last question is probably the most important one in the list to ask when facilitating the top executive team of a global multinational. Normally, such companies are broken up into business units, each of which has a mandate to do what is best for that area. Hence, the only place where decisions can be made to add other business units or apportion investment in a different fashion across the existing units is at that elevated level.

An example of insight gained from these questions came from a major food company we worked with. They had a product range that was limited to frozen foods. An analysis of global trends identified a growing demand for convenience foods – prepackaged meals aimed at people in the upper end of the market too busy at the office to get home in time to cook. After an examination of their capabilities, this company realised that they had the capacity to develop a new line to tap into this trend. They have since increased their product range, and very successfully too.

Another illustration concerns a boys' high school in South Africa that at the time of the conversation played cricket and rugby but not soccer. After much debate around a 'relevant product offering', it was decided to add soccer, with the consequence that the school now fields one of the top schoolboy teams in its province. Music has also become a much stronger part of their offering. Moving further afield to a middle-class suburb of Melbourne in Australia, the conversation among the municipal team revolved around the provision of more facilities for the elderly as the demographics in the area changed. For young and old alike, streamlining the product line to suit their needs is critical.

Product Chain

This is the *vertical* chain of processes from raw material extraction through manufacture and wholesale to retailing to customers. In some countries, it includes recycling as well, because legislation is demanding that companies are responsible for entire product life cycles. Questions aimed at unpacking the nature and value (or not) in your product chain include:

- Do you want to operate through the entire chain so that you have control from start to finish (like an oil company)? Do your competencies dictate that you should only operate in a particular link in the chain and try to dominate that link (like supermarkets)?
- If you are an upstream producer, are there opportunities to go downstream and add value to your product offering before selling it?
- If you are a downstream producer, might you wish to go upstream to control some of your raw material sources?
- Are there constrictions in the product chain that are negatively affecting your offering? Can they be obviated?

A good example of the value of an analysis of the product chain came to the fore during our work with the executive team of a global tobacco company. Like most other tobacco companies, they operate across the entire product chain from growing the raw material (agricultural game), through manufacturing the product, to its retail and even out into numerous hospitality end-points. However, increasingly restrictive legislation surrounding the consumption of their product, together with other changes in the tobacco game, meant that the company's marketing arm had lost valuable access to consumers. The executive team realised that they needed to focus more attention on the final link in the product chain, i.e. the retail and hospitality outlets, if they were to regain any measure of control over their ultimate destiny.

Concentrating on operations downstream for this company required a re-allocation of resources, but for many companies such a move downstream or upstream in the product chain often requires the acquisition of competencies they may not possess. Tactics to do so may therefore include the investigation and development of joint ventures/alliances with companies that do have competencies in the areas being targeted. An instance of where this fact became glaringly obvious was a gold-mining company that wanted to add value to its product by going downstream into jewellery manufacture and retail. The vast difference between digging the stuff out of the ground and turning it into something that women want became apparent as soon as the mining executives of the one company met the jewellery design team of the other. Their clashing taste in clothes gave it all away.

A further scholarly example is a nice way to round off this section. At a session with one of the most select private schools in South Africa, the issue was raised as to whether the product chain should be extended backwards from the existing primary/secondary configuration to kindergarten/pre-primary as well. This would ensure that potential pupils would be captured in the system at the earliest possible age.

Market Segment

As the name implies, this part of a conversation profiles the segment of the market towards which your products or services are targeted. This can comprise industrial clients in business-to-business trade, or consumers, in which case the debate centres around such things as age, gender, income and lifestyle. Market segment may be a factor that directly or indirectly influences your product or service offering. To this end, sub-questions that you should ask include:

■ Have there been changes in the demographics of your market which may increase or reduce demand?

- Have there been advances in technology affecting consumer behaviour in your market, e.g. the shift to downloading music off the internet by young people, the shift to internet banking or the shift to purchasing airline tickets off the internet? Do these shifts necessitate a change in your product/service offering and/or create the need to exploit other markets?
- Are there shifts in the spending power between different layers of society which favour your products or mean you will have to capture completely new customer groupings?
- Have there been psychological shifts in the market segment that could influence consumer taste for your products and services?
- If you have one industry as a dominant client, what are the prospects for that industry in terms of future demand or regulation or anything else that might have a significant impact? Should you be looking elsewhere to diversify your risk?
- Does your brand still match the changing playing field? Is the message conveyed in your brand still relevant? Can you expand your market segment through rebranding or developing a new, associated brand? Think of BMW, a brand that was very niched in the upper income and slightly older group. When they wanted to increase their market segment, the company decided the best way was to capture a younger market with the same aspirational values that might lead them on to the BMW brand. So they released a new brand – MINI.
- Are the Chinese an existing player or a potential new entrant in your market segment? What is your game plan to compete with them if they regard your space as their space? It may be the moment to move on to another space or join up with them.

An interesting example of how shifting demographics within a market segment has impacted on a product is in play in South Africa. Focused policies by the government, changing regulations and a growing economy have produced a burgeoning sector of new homeowners, especially in the lower end of the market. People owning these homes need to paint their homes; but they don't own cars and instead use public transport, and paint is not the easiest thing to transport. So a re-examination of the packaging of paint products and route to market has become necessary for paint manufacturers.

One of the banks which used our conversation model recognised that their elite image at the time was out of step with the realities of the new South Africa and the rise of the black middle class. They have since rebranded themselves to offer wider appeal and be seen as a bank with all the nation's citizens at heart, especially the next generation of entrepreneurs. But what this case illustrates is the importance of involving the advertising agency at an early stage to ensure that their campaign reflects any changes in the company's strategic objective concerning market segment.

Geographical Footprint

The geographical footprint is defined by the following two questions:

- Where do you want your business to be located?
- Where do you want to market and sell your products or services?

The answers to these questions differ considerably, depending on whether you are a large or a small business. For a small business, geographical footprint is normally a question of whether you want to be a local business servicing a particular town or region or whether you want to go further afield and establish a national footprint or at least a footprint in all the major cities in a country. You may need to spread your production network to achieve this and open up multiple offices; or maybe there is a distribution network you can use which can be satisfied by one production source. The biggest difference between the past and the present for small business is the internet. You literally can market your product anywhere in the world off your website – something which would have been impossible to do twenty-five years ago.

For medium to larger companies which already have a national footprint, the issue is whether you wish to establish businesses in other countries. One of the principal reasons for spreading your wings in this fashion is to diversify economic and political risk. This can be done by having revenue-generating bases in a variety of countries or regions that act independently of each other. Of course, such a strategy does not take the risk of a global slump out of play, but it does protect you against specific national risks. Another reason obviously is to expand your market generally if you have a product or service you believe can be sold elsewhere. While exporting from your home country is a perfectly reasonable option, it often requires a physical presence in other countries to trigger sales (particularly if they are inclined to protect their home industries with quotas or tariffs). In our experience, one of the strategies that has to be considered by South African companies is to use home-grown competencies to push into selected African countries now that the continent to the north is opening up for business. An easy way to do this if you are a service company is to follow your client's footprint if that client is beating an expansionary path into Africa. One of the banks we did scenarios for has merged with a British bank in order to take advantage of the latter's African footprint (while the British bank wanted to re-establish its presence in South Africa).

Multinationals that operate across many countries often prefer to manufacture their products in countries with a relatively low cost of manufacturing (e.g. China) and then sell these products into developed markets. This may make business sense, but the cost and logistics of transporting products from point of production to the market is something that needs to be considered. What must also be borne in mind is the possibility of nasty geopolitical scenarios, which could disrupt international supply lines. Global warming could moreover mean higher freight charges as carbon emissions are figured into the cost of transport.

If you only dominate the market in one country, it is critical to understand who else may put their footprint beside yours (particularly if the foot belongs to a global giant). Look at South African Breweries in the 1980s. As a wholly South African operation, it had dominated the local market during a time when international companies were discouraged from investing in South Africa. As the country moved towards a more democratic status and was embraced globally, SAB was suddenly faced with the prospect of competing with international companies on its home turf. The company had two options – stay focused on a local market and fight tooth and nail to try and hold onto market share or, if it wanted to create sustainable growth, expand internationally. The company's decision was the latter with the first countries targeted being in Eastern Europe. Old and rusting breweries were acquired and upgraded to SAB standards. Then came the moves into the US and China. Now, as SABMiller, it is one of the top three brewing companies in the world by volume.

The one caveat that should be offered in the conversation around expanding one's global footprint is the fact that countries can have very different rules of the game. Socratic logic is different from Confucian logic! Hence, many well-managed companies have come unstuck when they have invaded foreign lands and found the rules of engagement with the competition (and the government) to be totally alien to their normal way of doing things. It requires local savvy to make up for ignorance, and that usually comes in the form of a trustworthy local partner.

Here is a sample of responses we have had to the second question on scope:

When our national airline carrier decided not to pay commission on airline tickets sold by travel agents, we knew that other airlines would follow suit. We realised that our business model was no longer valid and that our primary product was no longer the focus of the business. Customers could now book airline tickets directly with the airlines or on-line via the internet. We were about to be disintermediated from the chain! In order to survive and add value to the chain again, our primary product became the specialised advice we offered through our extensive knowledge of the travel industry. If we hadn't changed our playing field, we'd now be off the field completely. CEO, NATIONAL TRAVEL GROUP

With the new regulatory laws in some countries around smoking coming into play, our initial thought was to look for new, emerging markets where growth could continue. This, however, was shortsighted because these laws are becoming accepted and implemented in more and more countries. Our primary focus is now to produce harm-reduction tobacco products, or new smokeless tobacco products. In order to do this, though, we will need to allocate far more resources to R&D than in our current model.

CEO, GLOBAL TOBACCO COMPANY

In many countries, beneficiation of raw materials before exporting them may become a rule of the game. Have we got the core compe-

tencies to move into this aspect of the product chain or will we need an alliance partner who does? EXECUTIVE, GLOBAL MINING GROUP

Today's schools need to strategise in order to attract pupils. Schools ought to offer a product that uniquely differentiates them in some form. Most schools become known as rugby, cricket or hockey schools, but we have chosen to define our playing field as offering a 'generalist education'. It fits with the community in which we serve, and offers a holistic, well-balanced approach to education.

PRINCIPAL, LEADING CO-ED HIGH SCHOOL

We were a property group known for its premium focus at the top end of the residential property market. With the recent shift in the demographics in the country and the rapid expansion of a middle class, we were losing sales in the mid-sector. We have since shifted our playing field and subtly redefined our brand. We now sell across nearly all market segments, but still offer a premium service.

CEO, RESIDENTIAL PROPERTY GROUP

Maize is a commodity, grown as a food source around the world for humans and for animals. However, rising energy demand, combined with the issue of global warming, have brought biofuels to the fore. Maize is a good source for ethanol. This has opened up a completely new market segment for us and will undoubtedly lead to higher prices. We will be feeding tanks as well as mouths.

MAIZE FARMER

We have changed the scope of our game completely from farming crops and animals to running a game farm. We don't have to rely on weather like we used to and we have lots of overseas tourists flocking to our place. We advertise in most European capitals with the by-line: "Come and see the Big Five without catching malaria." Hypochondria definitely works in favour of our new enterprise.

GAME FARM OWNER

We produce high pressure hoses for exploration companies to keep their drill holes clean. Somebody had the bright idea that another market segment could be fire stations and associated emergency services. With a small amount of capital to make the necessary conversions, we now supply a growing and highly profitable US market.

CEO, DRILLING EQUIPMENT COMPANY

Our playing field is divided into two halves. The one half can be explained by the fact that we are short of resources other than coal. So in that half of the field, the game is to do deals with all the countries in the world that have resources – particularly African countries. The other half of the field is focused on turning those resources into manufactured products at a competitive price using Western brands and Western technologies. We now have one of the most open economies in the world, a trillion dollars of foreign exchange and a growing capacity to move from replication to innovation. The next phase of the game is to create our own original products and global brands; and to establish a private equity fund to buy into foreign players of interest.

CHINESE ACADEMIC, BEIJING

Obviously our core activity is teaching the Word of God and ministering to the religious and spiritual needs of those in the community that want to come to our church. But in our country, the scope of the church's activity has to be extended to cater for the social needs of people including those infected and affected by HIV/AIDS. The problem is we don't at present have the resources, the infrastructure and the skills to establish a social responsibility function. We must start addressing this problem at this workshop.

ANGLICAN PRIEST, JOHANNESBURG

Widening your scope into a 'one-stop shop' is a real fad at the moment, but you have to be careful about what consumers perceive as a reasonable addition to your offering. As an example, 'bancassurance' hasn't worked that well because customers put

69

banking and insurance into separate compartments and expect dif-ferent service providers. On the other hand, preparation of a will can be part of a bank's bouquet.   MANAGER, RETAIL BANK

You must realise that academics by their very nature rule out 'rul-ing out'. Everybody at this session will fight their corner for the con-tinued existence of their faculty and all the programmes contained in it. And they'll want new courses as well. So, the scope of univer-sities, like the universe, will continue to expand.

UNIVERSITY PROFESSOR

I have been a dairy farmer beholden to the price of milk that, like the price of any commodity, behaves in a volatile manner. I have decided to go further downstream in the value chain, having just purchased two Spar Food franchises. I supply both my stores with my milk.   DAIRY FARMER

The scope of our town's offering to tourists is determined by the fact that we are an oasis in the middle of a desert. We are already testing the environment to its limits.

COUNCILLOR, ALICE SPRINGS, AUSTRALIA

For any urban renewal scheme to be successful, its scope should encompass four activities: making the inner city safe; keeping it clean; providing shops, restaurants and entertainment so that people can have fun in the city centre; and finding the right balance between offices and residential apartments to make it a 'mixed use' location.

URBAN PLANNER

If you want me as an environmentalist to take your product chain seriously, you must examine the energy needs and environmental impact of every single link in the chain from raw material input to disposal at the end of the product's life.

CANADIAN RECYCLING EXPERT

6 Players: Who are the players that can most advance or retard your strategy, and how should you handle them in future?

Bad men live that they may eat and drink,
whereas good men eat and drink that they may live.
SOCRATES, as quoted by Plutarch

Socrates recognised that our lives are affected by people whose influence can be positive or negative when he asked of the fox: "Having traced your destiny line from start to present, where should you go to now? But then the third question has to be: 'Who is for you, who is against you and who is neutral?' In seeking to clarify the direction you wish to take, you have to return to the principle of being part of an interconnected system."

Every game has players – otherwise it wouldn't be a 'game' – each of whom plays a different role in the course of the game in terms of its direction and outcome. The players are therefore more often than not the most interesting aspect of the game (think of the media coverage given to sports celebrities); and yet we generally don't spend enough time understanding an individual player's influence on the game. Business leaders are quick to talk about developing positive relationships with all stakeholders and seeking their views before decisions are taken. On the other hand, many haven't a clue about any of the other stakeholders' DNA – i.e. why they are what they are – which after all determines the latter's perception of the game. They gloss over the nature of the relationships required to be successful in the game on the grounds that they can meet their objectives without too much external assistance or interference.

Sometimes the absence of a critical examination of the other players is simply a consequence of being in a game for so long

71

that everything is taken for granted. This runs the risk of ignoring or missing another player's repositioning within the game as it changes. For as we have already stressed, games are continually evolving and so naturally do the roles and behaviour of the players. Part of analysing how a game has changed is therefore assessing how the other players have fared or modified their function and what new players have emerged. Failure to do this means that you can lose out on opportunities to leverage relationships with those players who will most gain from your winning; and to come up with defensive strategies against those players who will most gain from your loss.

The Perfect Fit

Management and political theorist Mary Parker Follett, who first coined the phrase 'conflict management', said in 1940 of relationships with players who could influence your game: "The nut and the screw form a perfect combination, not because they are different, but because they exactly fit into each other and together can perform a function which neither could perform half or alone or any part of alone." The relevance of this quotation increases with the growing interdependence of the players in both the political and economic games of the world today.

So, in your game, who are these players that will provide a perfect fit? Are there enough of them within your organisation? Do they exist elsewhere in the game? How can you draw on their expertise to benefit you? How can you stop the opposition achieving a perfect fit before you do? Top coaches in a match of soccer, for example, know the attributes of all the players on both sides and how each person's play can contribute towards the outcome of the game. They know which individuals to draw on from the squad to get the best fit. They know which individuals shouldn't be picked together because they don't get along so well. They understand perfectly the influence a positive team dynamic can have on the result. Furthermore, they are not averse to adopting tactics which will sufficiently interfere with the other side to cause maximum discomfort and misalignment; and, importantly, working out how they can take advantage of such a reaction and score extra goals.

Each step, or move, you make in a game cannot be undertaken without thinking of the ramifications it will have on the other players. As the fox quite correctly remarks to Socrates: "So you have to weigh up your friends and enemies and those who can go either way before deciding on your next move? I like that, because in the animal kingdom you very quickly learn who is out to kill you and who isn't. You avoid the places where the former may be and stick to potentially friendly territory." Of course in the game of business, things aren't so clear. Socrates explains it thus: "With human beings it's more difficult to judge, for we have the quality of deceit. But nothing really happens unless you have a few or many people on your side and you find ways around those whom you have identified as obstructing you." Unlike sport, where the rules of straight competition apply (for me to win, you have to lose), business is about collective wealth generation. Yes, there is competition – but no, it is not a good thing to destroy all the other players in the game and then become a monopoly yourself, taking advantage of your pre-eminent position in the process. Society won't benefit from that result and consequently there are social and ethical rules of engagement covering the world of commerce, which we will describe in the next chapter.

While the influence that external players have on the game is often overlooked in traditional planning sessions, the same applies to ourselves as players. Successful companies tend to underestimate how much their presence may have changed the game. This is dangerous because it means they risk overlooking how other players see them and may wish to react to narrow the gap. As an example, a small company that grows into a major player that dominates the game can shift from being perceived as a worthy opponent to becoming a target for populist attacks. Microsoft is a case in point, but so is Google. Too much success changes your appearance from innovative crusader to exploiting colossus in the blink of an eye. As the Chinese say, "Nail that stands up going to get hammered down."

Yet more worrying than being a dominant player who changes the game is being a player who is at the mercy of others. If it's not you influencing the game, then who is? Analysing all the players in the game is important, but what is *essential* is to stand back and identify the few *key* players whose decisions and actions may be transforming the nature of the game. These players need to be carefully monitored because you have two choices – copy them or come up with something different that is even better.

Referees and DNA

Where sport and business do coincide is in the fact that players are never free from scrutiny by referees. After all, every game has rules and therefore requires constant supervision to ensure that players do not break the rules. Although in some countries business games are governed more closely than others, every country has its referees, whether they are government ministers, civil servants, regulatory bodies, state-appointed committees or ombudsmen. The function of these 'players' (because in our methodology we classify them as such) is to ensure that the game moves smoothly along, is continually evaluated and, where it is in danger of going off the rails, restored to normality. Referees can play an important role in determining the outcome of the game because the job demands a balancing act of note. Too much officiousness (for that read bureaucracy) and the flow of the game is spoilt; too little and things can get out of hand with players adopting unconventional (and sometimes unfair or illegal) tactics to gain advantage or create pandemonium. Consequently, referees require a thorough understanding of the game before they are appointed – or in the case of a government, elected.

Nevertheless, a critical difference between referees and government is that the former are only there to interpret the rules whereas the latter in important aspects of the business game are rule-makers. They enact laws on commerce, fix tax rates, provide subsidies and other incentives, etc. Moreover, business games need an extra dimension of care and control, since they normally involve the livelihoods of a majority of a nation's population. The relationship between the key players is more complex than sport, and no business game is perfect in its design and outcome. As we've already mentioned, for a game to be sustainable, pure competition with a definitive end point of a victor and vanquished can never be the sole imperative. On the other hand, as soon as government starts protecting its players from foreign competition, other governments will follow suit. So you have to rely on a balance, specifically a balance between free markets (globalisation) and the societal objectives of individual nations (like a 'better life for all' in South Africa). This demands a level of co-operation between governments to stop the international game becoming distorted, either because some countries don't really understand the rules or deliberately cheat with an eye on short-term results.

Players can be prioritised according to their importance in your game. But for all of them, an understanding of their 'DNA' is critical – particularly if they are foreign players. Let us revisit this concept of DNA. Despite globalisation which has been accompanied by mass consumerism so that to some extent we all wear the same clothes, drink the same drink, watch the same TV programmes and go to the same movies, important and critical differences between national cultures remain. It's in our bones; it's in our blood; it's fundamental to the way we view the world. That's just the 'nature' side of the equation. On the 'nurture' side, our parents, our position in society (class), the schools we attend, the communities we live in – in short our environment – also affect our DNA. We can see Socrates and the fox figuratively nodding their heads in agreement!

Now in a sport like athletics, these differences don't really matter as it's all about physical prowess. Even in chess, a non-Russian sometimes becomes world champion. But in business if you wish to engage properly with all the other players in your game, you must acknowledge the differences and try to understand how the other side ticks. This applies equally to competitors and members of your own team. Only then will you be able to optimise your strategy and tactics. So we must now return to our original Socratic question: who are the players for you in the game that want you to win; who are against you and want you to lose; and who are neutral and liable to swing either way? Within this framework, a range of sub-questions can be asked in regard to a specific category of players such as competitors, suppliers, customers, employees, governments, communities and shareholders. Examples follow.

Competitors

Very few companies profile the competition during a strategic session. We insist that they do so by posing these questions:

- Who are your main competitors?
- What is different about their DNA compared to yours and in what respects are they stronger or weaker?
- In particular, how big are they in relation to you?
- What do you think their assessment is of you as a player?

By keeping your main competitors on the radar screen, you will be continuously aware of any changes they are causing to the game and you will note the entrance of new players and the exiting of unsuccessful ones. Such information brings with it insight into any changes in your position within the game in terms of relative size and influence. A big gorilla with greater economies of scale can just as easily kill you off as a swarm of bees with no overheads. Indeed, in our facilitations, we have come across so many examples of medium to small-sized businesses battling it out with the big guys. To continue the metaphor, if you are a mid-sized orang-utan up against a 400-pound gorilla, you have three options: exit the game; become a 'boutique orang-utan' and differentiate yourself from the gorilla; or marry the gorilla (or a group of other orang-utans to become a gorilla). As for the bees, best to leave them alone. You'll never beat the price of the honey they deliver in their own game.

Suppliers

Supply chain excellence is all the rage these days. It involves meeting your suppliers/subcontractors outside the normal negotiating period when the relationship is usually focused on price (and is naturally combative). The reason is to establish a rapport and develop a mutual understanding of each other's game and DNA. Much money can be saved this way as the parties adjust their practices to each other's realities. Because networking is about people, you should have a special contact person at each of your suppliers to whom you can pick up the phone anytime.

So the sort of questions we raise around suppliers are:

- Who are your key suppliers and are they assisting you in winning the game. Are you, for example, their sole client, or do they supply your competitors as well?
- When did you last have a heart-to-heart conversation with your suppliers about your respective games?
- What are their strengths and weaknesses and what significant risks if any do they face (remember you inherit all of these as you are downstream of them)?
- Are any of your suppliers malfunctioning and causing your business real grief? If so, what are the alternatives?
- What criteria do you use in choosing your specific suppliers? Is it pricing, quality, consistency of delivery, service excellence, treatment of their employees and ethical standards generally, track record on the environment, health and safety, or a combination of all these?
- Are some of your suppliers larger than you and taking advantage of it by using their negotiating clout to squeeze the extra cent? Do you treat the smaller ones well by paying them promptly and having simple tender procedures?
- What is the turnover rate of your suppliers? In other words, do you have long-term stable relationships built on trust or do you try to keep your suppliers on their toes by chopping and changing them?

Of course, an additional question that is put to suppliers in South Africa concerns the credentials they possess in the area of black economic empowerment. This counts towards the 'empowerment scorecard' of the company putting out the tender and procuring the goods. Interestingly, the strategy of

Chinese companies is to form long-term relationships with their key foreign suppliers (countries and companies), especially those providing raw materials. All in all, strategic negotiation has become an increasingly important skill for players in today's global game where the type of relationship you ought to cultivate with your suppliers is of the two-way, symbiotic kind (as opposed to the one-way grab-it-all variety).

Customers

There's a bit of role reversal going on here since, as a supplier to your customers, they are entitled to ply you with the questions of the previous section. Nevertheless, you ought to have questions for them and about them as well:

- Who are your major customers? If they are businesses, what do you know about their game? If they are end-consumers, have you worked out their DNA so that you can second-guess what they want next?
- Do you regularly vet your customer call centres since, as the front-line link to the public, they can do irreparable harm to your brand if they are inefficient and rude?
- When did you last do a customer survey to see what they think of you and particularly where they believe improvements can be made to your products or service?
- In the event that you are expanding or changing your market segment, what is the DNA of the potential customers in the new area (this question applies especially where a company is introducing a premium brand catering for high income/high net worth individuals)?
- Should you be an exporter, do you cater for the different DNAs of the different nationalities of your consumers in the design and promotion of your products?

Generally speaking, markets continually change and are one of the driving forces behind changes in the game. Demographics play an essential role in changing the customer base and should therefore be monitored for any shifts that could impact on the game. For instance, most European countries are experiencing a 'geriatric boom', which signifies a growing market for products and services for the elderly. If you are to build a sustainable relationship with your customers you need constantly to ask where your customer sees value and whether or not you are providing, and thereby tapping into, that value.

Employees and Unions

Internally, these are the most important players. As such, a trio of questions to kick off this section with are:

- Are your employees for you or against you or just plain neutral?
- Do they enthusiastically buy into your organisation's philosophy or do they just come to work in an uninterested fashion?
- Are you aware of how different the post-yuppie generation are to the young people recruited 10 or 20 years ago, and have you adapted your management systems accordingly?

It is amazing how many executive teams of companies we have facilitated put their employees in the 'neutral' category. How on earth can you expect to win the game if you don't have a positive team dynamic? After all, it is essential for victory in team sports. Tactics that can be chosen to improve employee morale and alignment include bonus and promotion schemes based on the company's meaning of winning the game; employee share-ownership schemes; regular briefings on strategy; and allowing them to have conversations like these and taking the results seriously.

It may be advisable to break this group down for further analysis into, for example, the young talent (novices, apprentices and new employees); older employees with long service; retirees who work as part-time consultants; the families and dependants of employees; top/middle management; shop floor staff; shop stewards and other union officials. In the end, they all have to get along and think the organisation is worthwhile. Otherwise, defeat by opposition companies becomes a genuine possibility.

The other really crucial question to ask about employees is: what type of culture do you have in the organisation, and does it match the game and how you want to play it? If you are a multinational operating in a variety of countries, the relationship between expatriate managers and local staff may demand particular care, given the different DNAs of the two groups.

To illustrate the pivotal nature of employees as players, we were called in to help a major bank which was dramatically losing market share. They realised the cause of their misfortune was obvious: all of the players in the game were neutral or against them. Their employees were situated in neutral, and so were their suppliers and customers. Their competitors were anything but neutral in gloating over their disarray! The bank's leadership knew they could never win until the 'neutral' were converted to 'for'. How did they achieve that? They walked the talk at all the branches with an inspirational message for employees, and cemented closer relationships with suppliers/ customers.

It goes without saying that trade unions, where they exist, are critical players. The worst thing to do is treat them in a disparaging manner because they can seriously disrupt your organisation with strikes and go-slows. Better to keep them updated on your plans in a way that does not compromise their or your independence.

Government and Parastatals

Every organisation has to play by the rules of the country in which it operates. So, as we mentioned earlier, government is another key player that demands careful analysis. But, of course, government can be broken down into tiers and departments, all of which can affect your game in one way or another. There's national/federal government, provincial/state government and local/municipal government. Then there's the Department of Finance, Department of Trade and Industry, etc. It is essential to distinguish between the government players who indirectly affect your game and those who have a direct bearing on it. With the latter, you need an ongoing relationship because they can make your game unplayable if they are unreasonable.

Parastatals too have a major impact on the game. If they don't perform in crucial areas of the game involving infrastructure and services, e.g. ports and airports, railways, electricity, water, etc., the private sector player can be up a gum tree without a ladder. In a democracy, no one should underestimate how significantly and quickly a newly elected government can change the rules. They can facilitate a game by, say, encouraging international investment or removing barriers to trade. At the same time, and in similar ways, they can inhibit the game by erecting new barriers or being heavy-handed with legislation. The government is invariably a hard player to deal with and with which to build a relationship. It doesn't consider itself a business in a free-market economy; nor should it, because its agenda is not driven by profit, but by wider societal considerations. A word of caution, though, which should never be forgotten: politicians play a political game and business CEOs would be wise to have a grasp of what it entails.

Communities and NGOs

Even though some managers never look over the fence, businesses do not operate in a spatial vacuum. They are located within a geographical space, the communities around which are genuine players. Yet communities are so often ignored. Whether the physical unit is a factory or a mine or the head office of a business that is the hub of economic activity in the area, a friendly milieu in which to operate is a major bonus – the opposite a major liability. Think of how much difference the attitude of the fans makes to a team's performance in a game of soccer. That's why 'home' games are easier to win than 'away' games. Home for business is the community around it; they are the ones who pack the stadium. Best to have them as your fans cheering you on than cheering for the other side.

Communities can *inter alia* be classified into local residents living in villages/towns/cities near company sites, residents associations, chambers of commerce, schools and universities, hospitals, small businesses that are potential suppliers, NGOs and special interest/pressure groups. Of course, the local municipal authorities feature in this list too. Corporate governance (running your company ethically), corporate social responsibility (caring about the environment, health and safety) and corporate social investment (financially supporting worthy local causes) are becoming hot potatoes, given the increasing trend to look at business as more than an economic actor. Communities are beginning to wield more influence because they know this and how their actions can enhance or damage a company's reputation. They can actively shift some of the local rules of the game and the way business has to be transacted to be seen as responsible. In industries such as mining and agriculture that can have a serious impact on the environment, communities are becoming key players in the game since their approval has to be sought before the project is undertaken.

Whether one is looking at communities or NGOs, there are two real questions to ask above all others: who is the champion who gets things done and what can we do to assist? Where there is no champion, proceed cautiously, particularly when large amounts of money are being requested. The fox would heartily agree with this sentiment, since foxes are prone to action, not words. They respect like-minded types.

Shareholders

Despite the triple bottom line (profit, planet, people) being very much the phrase in vogue for all the reasons we've just cited, scratch the surface of many CEOs and you'll find a single-mindedness about the company's financial performance and growth in share price underneath. Consequently the shareholders are indisputably important players – especially as senior management are usually shareholders themselves through the award of either options or shares. The key questions are:

- Where do your shareholders in general stand? Are they for you, against you, or neutral? (Naturally, the answer depends very much on your performance as management.)
- Do you have a major shareholder/shareholders and what is your relationship with them? (They can frustrate capital expenditure plans by voting against them at meetings of the Board or shareholders.)

84

- Are there divisions between your major shareholders? If so, what are you doing to resolve the matter?

There can be few things more frustrating than having activist shareholders who don't share your vision. It makes playing the game extremely difficult. Are you communicating well or badly with them? It makes all the difference. Some companies we have worked with have been in the unenviable position of having shareholders who are competitors in the game. This presents all sorts of difficulties in terms of resource allocation and conflict of interest. Members of the public who are shareholders tend to be skewed towards short-term results, be it dividends or increase in shareholder value. They also wield considerable power over a business because they can vote to boot directors off the Board. Sometimes, it's hard to concentrate when such a sword of Damocles is hovering over your head! This partially explains the flurry of private equity deals that have recently been concluded, whereby companies are delisted and put into private hands again – friendly private hands (to begin with at least).

Other Players

Other players to identify and examine your relationship with include:

- *Nonexecutive directors* where you are the executive team. They wield considerable power over strategy these days. They appoint the CEO.
- The *media*, who are influential in shaping and swaying the perceptions of all other players, notably consumers. Specific media players are your own media spokespersons and columnists and reporters who specialise in your field. Questions you should ask include:

- Do you have a sufficiently open relationship with key analysts and role players within the media, and do they really understand your game (so that the reporting of it is accurate)?
- In case of emergencies and crises, do you have contingency plans in place for the media, bearing in mind that reputations are won or lost in the way you handle the media in the first 24 hours?

- The *investment community*: Here we are specifically referring to the pension funds/mutual funds, the stockbrokers, commercial banks and merchant banks – all the players in the money game. Are you on good enough terms to get new money when you need it?
- *Industry associations/representative bodies:* These bodies are vital in promoting the interests of the industry as a whole – it's the one opportunity of validly co-operating with your competitors! They also act as the interface with that crucial player – the State. Are they doing the job properly?
- *Advertising agencies:* Technically, these fall under 'suppliers', but they are so important because they are responsible for promoting your brands. As we've already implied, the agencies should be on the inside in terms of strategy so that brand campaigns are harmonised with it.

When facilitating a strategic conversation, we find companies often run through this section quite quickly. To them, it simply involves listing and clarifying the players in the game. The reality is that a thorough understanding of who the players are, and how they can influence the game, will feed into many of your strategic decisions. You should therefore take the time carefully to analyse the players, not only because your company is just one player in the game, but also because the rest will determine to a large extent whether you win or lose in the end. Of course, there are superstars who rely on no one but themselves, but most of us need 'a little help from our friends' (to quote the Beatles).

We have done sessions with many other types of organisations besides businesses; but we don't have the space to list all the players for all the different sorts of organisations. Nevertheless, two entities merit further consideration. We have worked on scenarios for a number of countries, facilitating strategic conversations with a diverse array of stakeholders, e.g. China, South Africa, Zimbabwe, the Democratic Republic of Congo and Jamaica. Here the players look a bit different. Hence, we suggest that they are divided into internal players (those within the country) and external players (those operating on the global playing field). The list then looks something like this:

- Internal players including government, opposition parties, business and the private sector, NGOs and civil society, communities, etc. Obviously, a vital player is the individual citizenry and whether they are in harmony or at war with one another. Manchester United are a winning side because they are 'united'. Is your nation the same?
- External players including other countries, regional trading blocs, global bodies such as the WTO, UN and IMF and international business, etc. Does your nation get the support it should?

A strategic imperative for a country to succeed in the global arena is to have an aligned and winning team that can contribute something unique as an international player. It boils down to developing the requisite variety of expertise to match the natural strengths of the country concerned, while satisfying some niche in the demands of the world economy. Healthy

87

growth in GDP does not necessarily depend on size of economy or population; but it does depend on how responsibly the economy is managed by the government. The Head of State and Finance Minister are principal players in this game; and they have the intelligence agencies to keep watch on the other players!

On the other end of the spectrum to a country lies the family unit. They have a totally different set of players in their game, even if there's no family business involved. In terms of internal players, just ask yourself:

- Does my family operate as a team; or are we totally dysfunctional, with each member going his or her separate way and positively acting against the interests of the others?
- If it's the latter, is there no room for a conversation at the kitchen table?

As far as external players are concerned, these can stretch all the way from relatives, friends and work colleagues to your banker, doctor, employer, teacher, what have you. As in business, you should examine all relevant players and make up your mind whose side they're on and where the imbalances in your life are! How the players at home interact with you, and you with them, will certainly shape your personal game and influence the direction of your destiny line. It's a known fact that Socrates did not get on well with his wife. Perhaps she didn't appreciate the Socratic method of dialogue. His sons, though, supported him during his trial.

Now for some of the comments made in our workshops on players. Any sporting legend will tell you how important this phase of the conversation is:

Our major shareholders are a problem. Two of the three are actually our competitors and one has no interest in our industry. Strategically we need to address this situation urgently.

CEO, BEVERAGE GROUP

Our biggest competitor is the pharmaceutical industry. They are supporting the antismoking lobby because it gives them the opportunity to promote their own products that claim to help smokers give up smoking. However, they wouldn't want us out of the game; otherwise there'd no longer be any demand for that particular product segment. It is an interesting balance in the game.

EXECUTIVE, MULTINATIONAL TOBACCO MANUFACTURER

In the healthcare industry, the general practitioner used to be the gatekeeper. This has shifted and now it is the medical aid companies that hold the cards in the industry. This is where we need to build our relationships.

EXECUTIVE, HEALTHCARE AND PHARMACEUTICAL COMPANY

Looking at the future of the nonferrous metals industry in the European Union, two players are key to our future, and they both pose a threat – China because its industrial policy is different to Europe and it considers itself an independent player at all times; and the developing world which, as our key raw material supplier, are currently 'for' us. However, they are all on a beneficiation drive and could therefore soon be competing directly with us.

OFFICIAL, EU BODY REPRESENTING THE NONFERROUS METALS INDUSTRY

The government has become a player that seems to be firmly against us. It no longer understands the pharmaceutical industry and the need to make profits to fund research on new drugs. Instead, it is creating great uncertainty by intervening inconsistently in our affairs. You feel like quitting the market.

EXECUTIVE, GLOBAL PHARMACEUTICAL COMPANY

International banks are now moving into our country and it is incredibly difficult to compete against them. Their resources and infrastructure are much bigger. We will need to marry a gorilla just to stay in the game or alternatively look towards niche markets.

CEO, INVESTMENT BANK

Our relationship with our current advertising agency is weak. We need to improve their strategic understanding of the shift in our business and the new products we are launching, or else we should consider a new agency. These guys are key players in our lives.

EXECUTIVE, INTERNATIONAL FOOD GROUP

We are a parastatal. Our main competition funnily enough comes from other parastatals. We are overlapping our offering of services to the market, with the result that we are now competing. Our mandates are not clear and abided by.

EXECUTIVE, SOUTH AFRICAN PARASTATAL

There are four players in our game: the West, because they supply the brands, the technologies and the lion's share of the overseas markets for our products; the developing world because they supply the natural resources and some of the markets; the Communist Party because it runs China; and the Chinese citizenry who are the hardest-working, most disciplined people you could hope for when growing the economy. A Chinese riddle explains why people work so hard here: "Why is porridge better than love? Nothing is better than love, but porridge is better than nothing."

CHINESE HONOURS STUDENT, BEIJING

We have three players of note in our game: our donors, our permanent staff and our volunteers. Of the three, donors are the most fickle, giving us more than we expect one year and nothing the next. We try and take this uncertainty out of play by widening the donor base.

CEO, NGO FOR CARE OF SICK CHILDREN

90

My restaurant is only as good as my suppliers. If they don't supply me with Grade A meat and vegetables, there's not much the kitchen can do about it. So I visit them often.   RESTAURANT OWNER

Given that some of our chemical inputs come from unregulated overseas markets, we are under much greater pressure to vet the upstream players in the fertiliser game. One incident of food poisoning due to our sprays could put us permanently out of business.   EXECUTIVE, FERTILISER COMPANY

High net worth housewives are the most important players in our game. They are the ones we want to attract to our food shop and pamper once they're inside. So we have to offer products of the highest quality and with impeccable environmental credentials. Price is also a factor but it doesn't beat a tantalising selection on the shelves. We even throw in some really exotic items that you can't buy anywhere else in the city to tickle their fancy.   MANAGER, RETAIL FOOD OUTLET

For years we have supplied the charts used to log the performance of equipment in the factory and even the progress of patients in ICU. But the advent of the paperless society brought on by advances in IT has changed all that. Simply put, you can't be an analogue player in a digital game.   MD, GRAPHICS COMPANY

The Chinese are the best team players in the world because of their spirit of collectivism. They can construct suburbs, roads and rail systems at a rate we just dream of in the West. Ideally, they should build 20 Londons in 10 years to get 200 million people off the land into new cities. That's a tall order even for them.   URBAN PLANNING CONSULTANT

7 Rules: What are the rules of the game that are likely to govern your strategy under all scenarios?

Could I climb to the highest place in Athens, I would lift my voice and proclaim: "Fellow citizens, why do you turn and scrape every stone to gather wealth, and take so little care of your children to whom one day you must relinquish it all?"
SOCRATES, as quoted by Plato

Every game has rules. They define the game and provide a framework through which, and within which, the game is played. Any parent of a teenager will know that the foregoing statements go completely against the grain of teenagers' thinking. Fortunately for teenagers, though, one of the rules in life is that they inherit what we have accumulated ahead of them (unless we go skiing – spending the kids' inheritance). We also say 'fortunately', because in the absence of rules there is only anarchy and, in an anarchical state, freedom is diminished. "Rules," teenagers might counter, "are meant to be broken." Well, if you break rules in sport, you are liable to get a red card and be sent off; break the rules in business and bankruptcy probably awaits you. However, unlike those in sport, the rules in business change over time and vary in space, i.e. from country to country and, even within the same industry, from culture to culture. Teenagers are wrong: the challenge is not so much to try and break the rules, but to try and understand them and keep up with the changes.

Changes in business rules are driven by the evolution of social, political and regulatory conditions surrounding the game. Technological advancement, disintermediation and intensifying competition can act as permanent change agents too. For our definition of business rules is wider than the normal legal definition. In our methodology, they also represent the 'driving forces' or 'predetermined elements' that we are fairly sure will govern the game under all scenarios. Like good strategy rules in and rules out certain activities relating to scope, good rules of the game rule in and rule out possible futures. It's of real value to narrow the 'cone of uncertainty' when looking forward. This the rules are supposed to do in a Socratic manner by eliminating all futures which contradict them. Having 360-degree vision is all very well, but in the context of formulating strategy such an approach merely serves to create confusion. It brings to mind the old saw: "Give me a one-armed economist, so he can't say on the one hand and on the other."

Written and Unwritten Rules

To make things even more challenging for the players within the game of business (as well as that of life), some of the rules are to a large degree subjective. They are, in a way, parameters as perceived and set by each player. Selection of the rules is, therefore, more of an art than a science. You must deduce the other players' rules as well. Expressed differently, just as there are rules that are determined by forces or factors outside of the control of any player, so there are rules decided by the participants themselves. The forces of nature and the principles of science are examples of the former, whereas laws laid down by governments and corporate codes emanating from the directorate are examples of the latter.

On a personal level, self-regulation (or self-control) is something we learn from our parents if they are wise enough to teach us. These rules, together with our DNA, help define the limits or bounds of acceptable behaviour. Such internal rules are supplemented by ones imposed externally by adults in authority over us. Flout the latter and we soon learn that punishment is the consequence. It is no different for a nation playing the global game or a company playing the business game. Both types of rules apply and lead to reward or punishment, depending on the level of compliance.

A further categorisation of rules can be into those that are written down in the statute books and those that appear nowhere. Seeking to identify the second type gives you the advantage, whether they happen to be your own rules to win or rules dictated by external changes in the business environment. They usually do not form a multitude. Just a few, unwritten rules can swing your destiny line either way in the short and longer term. It is therefore vitally important to uncover these rules faster than your competitor, especially in light of the dynamic nature of markets and the fact that changes in the rules fundamentally change the game. As we have often seen, many companies continue to play according to the 'old rules' only to realise too late that they are now defunct. This would be inconsequential if such misjudgments had minimal effect. But in the dog-eat-dog world of business, losing a competitive edge because of an unnoticed shift in the game can be the difference between success and complete failure.

Our line of argument is not far removed from the explanation given by the fox, that in his world "the rule is simple and all-encompassing: you do lunch, or be lunch. Straight competition. Survival of the fittest." The similarity with certain elements of human endeavour was not lost on Socrates, who replied, "In our world that rule exists in commerce and war." This would suggest that the only rule of the game in business is that of competition. To a large extent this is correct, but true strategic advantage does not hang on the single thread of a dogged determination to win. It comes from a more intricate understanding of the game. Indeed, Socrates then went on to say: "Nonetheless, I have spent all my philosophical hours on enquiring about another set of rules that should co-exist with the rule of competition. These relate to morality and goodness, but everybody has a different idea of what they are. I doubt whether we will ever reach agreement, but the quest must continue."

And then there are the ecological rules – three of them according to Captain Paul Wilson, co-founder of Greenpeace International in 1979:

- The rule of diversity. The strength of an ecosystem lies in the diversity of species within it. Weaken diversity and the entire system will be weakened and will ultimately collapse;
- The rule of interdependence. All of the species within an ecosystem are interdependent. We need each other;
- The rule of finite resources. There is a limit to growth because there is a limit to carrying capacity.

He quotes Albert Einstein who wrote: "If the bee disappeared off the surface of the globe, then man would have only four years of life left. No more bees, no more pollination, no more plants, no more animals, no more man." And then Wilson adds that around the world bees are disappearing in a crisis called Colony Collapse Disorder. So there you have it: the rule of the disappearing bumble bee. It gives us "just enough time to get a college degree to discover that everything you learned is relatively useless when sitting on the doorstep of global ecological annihilation". It kind of makes it a very important rule that trumps all others.

Based on Socrates' avenue of philosophical investigation and the sentiments of Paul Wilson, we have identified three kinds of rules that you need to inquire about in order to understand the DNA of the game you are in: namely, descriptive, normative and aspirational rules. They cover all aspects of engagement, whatever you do.

Descriptive Rules

These rules describe the game you're in and the constraints you are under. They include the laws of the land and the regulations or charters relating to your industry. In addition, cultural norms are among the unwritten, descriptive rules that need to be taken into account.

If complied with, the descriptive rules are what grant you a licence to operate in the country or countries in which your businesses are located. As explained earlier, these rules can differ from country to country, which emphasises the severe problems multinationals can run into when they think one optimal strategy exists for all markets. Strategies (and tactics) should differ from country to country according to the descriptive rules of the game within each country. For the corporate head office to strategise more effectively, the underlying business units or divisions operating in different end-markets should feed their strategies back into the corporate team instead of the typical top-down approach of the centre dispatching plans to operations in the end-markets, thereby constricting or confusing them.

How often have you heard from people in the field: "We are limited in our game because our corporate strategy dictates . . ."? Clearly the local companies cannot be extracting full value from their markets if such an attitude prevails. An example of this kind of miscalculation is found in the number of exceedingly well-managed South African companies – particularly in the retail sector – which have foundered in overseas markets. They just don't get it: the local rules are different, consumers are different, just about everything in the game is different. Another demonstration of this principle concerns companies looking to expand into Africa, with its extremely diverse set of national rules, traditions and cultures. Unless companies have a clear understanding of the descriptive rules of a specific country in which they wish to operate, they risk getting burned. There is no single set of rules for 'operating in Africa' outside of the fact the government is always a key player!

The second type of descriptive rules which need to be explored are those that set out the long-term forces governing your market or industry. They constitute the near-certain trends which you may have already uncovered in the opening section on context. They relate to demographics, technology, shifts in consumer preferences, changes in the competitive environment, in other words all the nonlegal, noncultural stuff which can be classified as 'givens' in the game in the foreseeable future.

Questions that need to be asked at this juncture in the conversation are the following:

- Have there recently been any changes in the descriptive rules that could seriously affect any part of your business?
- Are there likely to be further changes?
- What unique descriptive rules apply in the countries where you are doing business?

Normative Rules

These rules cover ethics, corporate governance, care for the environment, health, safety, general working conditions/wage levels of employees and corporate social investment, i.e. all the things your company *ought* to do. Normative rules should be universal for all countries (although in reality they are flouted in some). Should a company apply different standards in this sphere they risk their inconsistency being picked up by the media – society's moral watchdogs – and then being publicly castigated. Instances of this are the intense moral pressure put on global companies not to do business with South Africa during the days of apartheid and, today, pressure not to operate in the sad list of 'failed states' in the world which continue to violate human rights.

Normative rules are becoming more important in a world that is increasingly interconnected, has issues like global warming and boasts more socially aware consumers. Indeed, some normative rules are almost classified as licences to operate, along with the descriptive rules of the game. And yet for many companies driven solely by the quest for bottom-line profit, these normative rules are, at best, tolerated. This is a risky game to play because minimal compliance can encourage individual employees to flout the rules, often with dire consequences. Sometimes all it takes is a minor accident to turn the spotlight onto the entire operations of the company in question – something management would far rather do without!

Questions that should be asked around normative rules are the following:

- Is your track record in relation to safety, health and the environment improving or deteriorating?
- Are there any new normative rules in the pipeline in host countries?
- Have you got a 'code of conduct' and are all your employees aware of it?
- Is there anything you are doing which is in conflict with your professed values and how are you going to stop it?
- Is your level of corporate giving in line with international norms?
- Which countries in the world should you rule 'out of bounds' because their rules of the game clash with the (stricter) normative rules your company has laid down

for itself? This is a dilemma that faces a number of mining/exploration companies that want to operate in certain countries but cannot because of the skewed value systems of the regimes there. Such countries are then classified as 'no-go' areas – unless, to be cynical, the treasure trove is just too inviting. As they say in business: everything has a price!

An interesting shift in the interpretation of normative rules has come about through the activities of certain major players entering the global game, such as China. They have altered the global playing field in such a spectacular fashion that many Western players view the normative rules they currently apply as a real handicap to remaining competitive. For decades the global game was dominated by the West and underpinned by normative rules that reflected the prevailing cultures of the countries that made up the West. Now the game has moved East where the normative rules – despite their universality – are applied differently. The cost implications are huge and have already created considerable tension between the players. Ultimately, though, both sides will see the sense in levelling the playing field because no game is sustainable without a sufficient degree of harmony over what constitutes fair play.

To summarise, a company's values should be unpacked and explored at this point of the strategic conversation. They should be given teeth by conversion into the internal rules of the game that determine how the company operates. On every notice board should be displayed statements such as: 'We do not hire child labour'; 'We pay a living wage'. Think of the normative rules as the corporate equivalent of the Hippocratic oath, i.e. a private contract, not a legal one. Incidentally, Hippocrates – the most famous of Greek physicians – was a contemporary of Socrates.

Aspirational Rules

Aspirational rules are based on *your* understanding of the game and what *you* believe are the golden rules to *win* the game. They are usually few in number but critical for the sustainability of a company. For example, in the mining industry an aggressive acquisition policy and quality/longevity of ore deposits are rules to win – especially with the growth in global demand caused by China and India as they move through their respective industrial revolutions. Throw the scarcity – or the concept of scarcity – of commodities into the pot and mining suddenly becomes a very different game to what it used to be. The winners will be the companies that first instigated a modification to their aspirational rules in line with the new developments in the industry.

In many service industries, on the other hand, the rule to win revolves around the establishment of long-term relationships with clients based on trust and value for money. In one company that has just introduced a premium brand in its product range, the rule to win is to keep that brand separate and distinct from its other brands in the public consciousness. One of the better rules to win came from a bishop in the Anglican Church. "Entertainment rules even in the church," he said, adding for good measure, "pepping up our services is the only way to attract the youth back into our congregations."

In business, we all want to be world class and win the game. Some common aspirational rules seem to apply across the board, like the need for focus; strong branding and other forms of differentiation to make your product/service unique; benchmarking yourself against the other players and adopting global best practice; maintaining an entrepreneurial flair and a capacity for improvisation (difficult as a company gets bigger, but jazz concerts can still take place in large structures like the Royal Albert Hall in London); having a perpetual spirit of innovation (both incremental innovation to achieve operational excellence and radical innovation leading to a change in the game you play), and being fanatical about attracting, developing and retaining talented people.

Questions to be asked here include:

- What set of golden rules to win should your business adopt?
- How are you going to communicate these rules to all your staff?
- What key performance indicators should you introduce to measure progress towards complying with these rules?

American companies appear to be much better at articulating the golden rules than their counterparts in Europe or South Africa. Go into a McDonald's restaurant and every member of staff knows the rules on hygiene, service delivery and quality of product which will ultimately win them extra customers.

Conclusion

All the rules of the game – descriptive, normative, aspirational – should be taken into account when developing the options later on in the strategic conversation. In fact, the operational planning sessions that annually follow the strategic conversation should include tactics to lead you towards closer compliance with the rules. It has to be said that how you act in accordance with the rules is wholly within your control, whereas the rules themselves are part and parcel of the game.

Comments made when discussing the rules of the game comprise the following selection. Notice the diversity of games covered in terms of industries and countries:

In South Africa, the government has introduced black economic empowerment as a new rule. You have to have a BEE in your bonnet or you must go and play the game elsewhere. Initially it was an aspirational rule but now we have charters which have turned it into a descriptive rule. The aspirational rule therefore is to go beyond the level of minimum compliance, and be a leader in the industry.

CHAIRMAN, TRANSFORMATION COMMITTEE, MINING COMPANY

Even better to have bees with bonnets! FEMALE BANKER

In the property game in South Africa, a new descriptive rule is a higher set of qualifications for estate agents. Its intention is to lift the level of the game and to recognise that selling property should be conducted in a thoroughly professional manner.

CEO, LEADING PROPERTY GROUP

Our key aspirational rule is to understand our clients' needs and to build sustainable relationships with them.

EXECUTIVE, INVESTMENT BANK

An aspirational rule in supplying retail chains is to get the shelf space. Big suppliers use every means to get it, which gives them an unfair advantage. In addition, a descriptive rule some chains have introduced is that our products should carry the chain's brand name because they don't want customers to know that the produce is coming from different countries at different times of the year. It makes it difficult for us to differentiate ourselves. APPLE GROWER

Our diamonds are not forever! This is a rule of the game we must take cognisance of, seeing that our economy is reliant on diamonds. If we are to be viable in the future, we need to diversify into a whole range of other activities that have nothing to do with the diamond business. PUBLIC SERVANT, BOTSWANA

Europe adheres to high environmental standards and is committed to addressing issues around climate change. These normative rules put all European corporate players at risk by increasing their costs relative to companies in countries where the same conditions are not enforced. EXECUTIVE, EU INDUSTRIAL GROUP

The last man still standing in the resource game will win it! EXECUTIVE, MULTINATIONAL MINING GROUP

Professionalism, ethics and integrity are the DNA of our game. So all three types of your rules are in play all the time. SENIOR PARTNER, INTERNATIONAL LAW FIRM

There's a new rule of our game that can have potentially devastating consequences. As an account officer I am now accountable for any books I sign off, irrespective of who the client is. This means if there are any signs of wrongdoing on the part of the client, it is I who risks going to jail. So now our firm has to reassess our client base, be very sure of new clients, and understand their business well. SENIOR PARTNER, LEADING ACCOUNTING FIRM

We have three rules of the game. The first is guanxi, which in Chinese means connections. You are who you know. We were the first networking nation. The second rule is one child per couple which has been in operation for nearly 30 years. This is to stop overpopulation. The third rule we call 'Chinese baseball'. In American baseball the rules never change, but in our baseball the rules change during the game. CHINESE ENTREPRENEUR, SHANGHAI

In the motor vehicle industry, economies of scale and cost competitiveness are the aspirational rules of the game for the mass manufacturers. However, as a premium brand, we realised we could not compete in this arena; so we decided that our aspirational rule should play on the social aspect of owning/driving a car. We differentiated

103

ourselves by promoting a lifestyle experience. The car becomes the vehicle to achieve this.

SENIOR EXECUTIVE, EUROPEAN MOTOR VEHICLE MANUFACTURER

There are two rules of the game associated with holding a successful conference these days. The first is a prohibition on all overpaid foreign gurus. Most of them have passed their sell-by date in any case. The second is to avoid what we call the 'conference sluts' – speakers who will do anything to be put onto next year's list. I mean anything. CONFERENCE ORGANISER

We have six golden rules to clinch a transaction. All the sales people within our organisation know those rules and apply them. You watch! Before you've completed the facilitation of this session I'll have sold you a complete range of my company's cosmetics. And I'll have convinced you – even though you're a man – that you look much better with my products on than au naturel.

REGIONAL MANAGER, DIRECT MARKETING COSMETICS COMPANY

One of the rules of the game reigns supreme over all the others. Even if the rest of the grid goes down, never interrupt supplies to an aluminium smelter. The stuff freezes over before you can even say 'abracadabra'.

CUSTOMER CARE MANAGER, ELECTRICITY PARASTATAL

I quickly realised that a rule of the game in fighting organised crime in New York is to think like an Italian. That was no problem for me because I am of Italian descent. As a result we got serious crime down to levels last seen in the late 1940s. I hope you can do the same here in Johannesburg by putting yourself in the criminals' mind in order to defeat them. EX-MAYOR, NEW YORK

8 Uncertainties: What are the key uncertainties that could have a significant impact on the game and divert your course either positively or negatively?

Remember that there is nothing stable in human affairs; therefore avoid undue elation in prosperity, or undue depression in adversity.
SOCRATES

As the fox so wisely said to Socrates: "Life can surprise you and it is better to be aware of the surprises in advance or have a very fast reaction time if they really do come out of the blue."

In business, the saying goes that 60 per cent of a company's bottom-line profit comes from how quickly and effectively it responds to things outside of its control. Obviously, the basic idea of the business has to be well thought through and profitable; but it's how the idea is modified in light of changing market conditions that separates the sheep from the goats. For example, in the automobile industry Toyota is ahead of the game with its hybrid petrol/electric car called the Prius. It recognised before its competitors that people's attitude towards conservation of the environment has grown much stronger. And this was before *An Inconvenient Truth* starring Al Gore! Speed of response is the essence of competitive advantage in today's business world. Failure to respond quickly and effectively means that, at best, a company will be continually playing catch-up or, at worst, soon find itself knocked out of the game.

Thus a question we often ask of a company's executive team is the following: "Does your company have a sufficient degree of flexibility in its decision-making process to adapt quickly enough to significant changes in its circumstances?" We then follow this up with what is, in reality, a rhetorical question: "If your company could somehow foresee these changes, surely it would have an even greater competitive advantage?" Yet conventional strategic thinking often takes place around the assumption that the future is unknown and unknowable; or – the exact opposite – that with enough experts it can be captured accurately in a forecast.

The Wisdom of Wack

Pierre Wack, whom we have already mentioned in this book, had a different view. It was somewhere between these two extremes. He believed that the future could be known, albeit with vagueness and difficulty, if it was approached with a 'sufficiently searching gaze'. Think of peering intently ahead in a fog and, by interpreting the indistinct shapes, you can make out what particular objects they are. He suggested that if we were to highlight the key uncertainties that may impact on us in the future, the logic of working through the consequences of these events or circumstances would allow for more clarity of thought, and create a natural instinct for future possibilities. He honed the technique by going East to visit Indian gurus, spending long periods of time studying their art of meditation and how they contemplated the world around them. He would have had a fascinating debate with Socrates, because intuitive inference arising from meditating on the possibilities is not as satisfactory or as precise as rational deduction, but it is the most appropriate tool when dealing with the future.

Here's an example of what Wack was trying to get at. Someone we know was driving down the main road in a suburb of Cape Town when she heard the sound of firecrackers and looked out of the side window to see puffs of smoke accompanying the sound. She thought how odd it was to mount a firework display in the middle of the pavement. Then she saw four men running down the street to a getaway vehicle and realised that she was in the middle of a gun fight. She quickly turned the corner into a side road, having remembered the licence number of the vehicle that sped away. She wrote it down and handed it to the police who were by then at the scene of the crime. "What value would a scenario planner have added?" you might ask. The answer is that, by having such a person play the possibility in advance to her, she would have *immediately* recognised the danger of being hit by a stray bullet and taken evasive action a split second sooner. As it happened, it didn't matter and, to her great credit, she had the presence of mind to get the licence number. But things could have turned out differently. It's all about reading the signs correctly and putting an event into its proper context. That needs practice.

This explains why, when conducting a strategic conversation, we feel it is vital to examine key uncertainties, i.e. those uncertainties that will have a major impact on the business and affect the outcome of the game. This means that if and when a key uncertainty plays out it has already been considered; its potential impact has been evaluated; options and decisions have been identified to address the effects, and the necessary resources are allocated almost immediately to implement those decisions. The result? The very real chance of maintaining a proactive and influential position in the game. The alternative? Continually operating in a mode of crisis management, with short-term tactical skills to keep the boat in an upright position while negotiating the rapids.

Socrates makes an important point about uncertainty, which links into our argument, when he mentions: "What you are does not determine what you will be." The reality is that as uncertainties unfold they will affect us – just as we will affect them – and we, and the outcome of the uncertainties, will change accordingly. If we can consider these uncertainties from different perspectives and perhaps play them out in our minds or conversation, we may be empowered enough to move our destiny line in a direction which we would prefer above all others. As the Chinese say: "Every crisis is an opportunity." Remember, though, there are 'known unknowns' – things you know you don't know – and 'unknown unknowns' – things you don't know you don't know and never can prepare yourself for. The latter have to be handled with a mixture of gut feeling and instant reasoning.

The Radar Screen

When considering key uncertainties, it is important for one to prioritise their 'key-ness' by plotting them on the business equivalent of a radar screen. Such a screen serves as a continual frame of reference to assess whether or not an uncertainty is indeed turning into a reality and, if so, whether proper contingency plans have been put in place to mitigate the consequences or adapt to them.

One of our favourite quotes in this regard comes from A A Milne's *The House at Pooh Corner,* that famous children's book full of adult wisdom. Piglet asks Pooh a very pressing question whilst they are in the Hundred Acre Wood during a roaring gale: "Supposing a tree fell down Pooh, when we were underneath it?" After careful thought Pooh replies, "Supposing it didn't." Piglet is comforted by this. Clearly Piglet has the uncertainty on his radar screen whereas Pooh doesn't!

So how does a company capture possible changes in the environment and itself on a radar screen, and have an idea of the consequences should they materialise? We use two axes on a piece of graph paper, the vertical one representing the probability of an event and the horizontal one its potential impact. 'Blips' close to the origin (bottom left) are improbable and are considered to have a relatively low potential impact. They can hardly be described as 'key uncertainties' at this point in time. 'Blips' on the top right of the paper are quite probable and could have a major impact. Blips elsewhere on the chart are somewhere in between on both counts. We like to call the result a 'PI chart' because we are measuring probability and impact. Of course, as a company proceeds into the future like a battleship slicing through the ocean, the executive team can – like the officers on the bridge – review the chart to see whether any of the blips have moved and become more dominant in relation to the company's future. Sometimes a key uncertainty can become so 'certain' that it converts into a rule of the game.

Types of Uncertainties

Our primary classification of key uncertainties is into three types:

- *Shock events* such as a stock market meltdown, a flu epidemic or the disruption of oil supplies due to a terrorist attack; or, closer to home, an unwelcome takeover bid for your company;
- *Gradual threats* such as global warming or HIV/AIDS (the human species is not programmed to handle these as effectively as shock events, preferring fight-or-flight situations instead); and,
- *Volatile parameters* that are critical to the business such as swings in commodity prices, exchange rates or interest rates.

Superimposed on these three types of uncertainties are the areas from which they can emanate. External uncertainties can play out in the global, national or local arenas, and they can be financial, political, social, technological, legal or environmental. They can arise because of shifts in the market that make your industry obsolete or uncompetitive (think of how many games become unplayable and how many new ones open up as nations move from a manufacturing-based to a service-based economy). They can relate to excessive dependence on a single customer; or they can stem from competitor strategies. A dramatic example of the uncertainties we have in mind is that San Francisco and Japanese businesses face the constant threat of an earthquake. We would describe it as an 'environmental shock event'. A shock event but of a man-made kind is an electricity black-out. They are happening more often these days as infrastructure around the world ages and does not get replaced. Of course the contingency plan is buying your own generator! The development of blog sites on the internet, the advent of 24-hour TV news channels and the capabilities of the latest PCs/cellphones to capture any type of data constitute a gradual technological or market-related threat to the printed newspaper industry.

In addition, smaller companies may have *internal* uncertainties relating to CEO succession, lack of controls in the back office, shortage of technically qualified staff or other factors. Some of these should be picked up by the internal or external auditors if they are doing their job properly, since risk evaluation forms an essential part of their service offering.

Moreover, risk evaluation shouldn't just be seen in the narrow context of health and safety and the financial accounts. Actually, risk evaluation is about understanding the systemic risks to the business and how they may be interconnected, and overlap with one another. For instance, an uncertainty in consumer preferences can influence or lead to an advancement in technology which makes another technology or process obsolete. Political and economic uncertainties are usually interrelated. Hence, all uncertainties need to be identified, unpacked, debated and discussed before they can be correctly plotted on the radar screen. However, given the scope of key uncertainties that could affect a company, especially a large one, if every uncertainty was played out in a set of scenarios it would lead to analysis paralysis. By logically focusing on those with the highest potential impact (whatever their level of probability), it is possible for management to see where the real strategic issues lie and paint the scenarios accordingly. One point bears repeating: whereas external uncertainties are normally beyond your control, your response to alleviate the impact of these uncertainties *is* within your control and constitutes tactics.

Among the sub-questions that should be asked are the following:

- Is the uncertainty something you can tolerate or does it make the game unplayable? For example, Russian roulette for most people is an unplayable game because the possible downside of oblivion, by a bullet through the head, is too much to bear. It is an unacceptable risk. Is there a chance that in your game your company can experience oblivion, in which case it might be best to change the game now?
- What are the positive as well as the negative consequences for you if an uncertainty materialises into actual fact? Remember that many uncertainties affect all players equally, and the quality of your response can elevate your position in the game.
- What shock events, if any, would put you out of business altogether? Is there any probability whatsoever of an occurrence of any of these events? If so, what are the signs you should watch for, and what will you do about it if the signs start blinking red?
- In terms of gradual threats, is the cost of adapting to the

threat more or less than the cost of taking action to mitigate it or even eliminate it?

■ What is the current range of values from highest to low-
est that you think is possible for a volatile parameter (e.g.
the future price of a commodity)? When you have previously experienced such ranges, has the actual value of
the parameter in the period specified ever risen above
or fallen below the estimated range? (If it has, you'd better widen your current range.)

Here are some of the key uncertainties raised in our strategic
exercises. The list is quite long because we want to show you
how much the conversation changes gear at this stage. Imagination takes flight!

*We have a mandate from the national government to replace shacks
with proper housing units throughout the country by 2014. Ironically, it is also a key uncertainty as we have not yet formulated a
clear strategy nor mustered the resources to achieve this.*
PROVINCIAL GOVERNMENT SPOKESPERSON ON HOUSING, SOUTH AFRICA

*A worrying uncertainty we face is energy supply from Russia as well
as future access to raw materials (mainly from Africa).*
PARTICIPANT, EUROMETAUX WORKSHOP ON NONFERROUS METALS

*Being in the wine industry, one of the longer-term uncertainties
we have to factor into our plans is climate change or, at the very
least, a shift in rainfall patterns. Another uncertainty for us, because
we are a global player, is the image of South Africa as a wine-
producing nation around the world.*　MANAGER, WINE ESTATE

*One of our major uncertainties is future government policy and
pronouncements on obesity. Will it be treated like smoking?*
EXECUTIVE, GLOBAL FROZEN FOOD MANUFACTURER

The future relationship of China with us and the rest of Africa is a key uncertainty, since China is emerging as the largest bidder for resources and land on the continent. In fact, you could say that Africa is up for sale; and we could all go under the Chinese hammer (never mind the sickle) in a scenario called 'Going, Going, Gone'.

PARTICIPANT, SCENARIO WORKSHOP ON SOUTH AFRICA

Given the level of economic hardship in Zimbabwe, is widespread internal unrest an uncertainty? I am not sure, because people have an incredible capacity to suffer in silence there. Nevertheless, everybody has a tipping point.

PARTICIPANT, SCENARIO WORKSHOP ON ZIMBABWE

We have always talked of 'above-the-line' and 'below-the-line' activities in the advertising industry. The former relate to the formulation of TV, radio or print ads and the latter to packaging, event promotion and point-of-purchase display. Now that we live in such a fragmented world where people are distracted by so many choices, is such a distinction relevant? This is creating great uncertainty among agencies about what their core functions are.

EXECUTIVE, ADVERTISING AGENCY

Political factors and traditional forms of land ownership in Africa sometimes make the securing of development rights and land tenure a hazardous business. In other words, property rights can be a key uncertainty, which is pretty fundamental to the success of any transaction.   CEO, LEADING PROPERTY DEVELOPMENT GROUP

The price of gold is, without a doubt, our main uncertainty. In terms of what makes it move, it's like a guard's van. You never know which freight train it's going to be hitched to next. That's what makes it such an exasperating, yet alluring metal. It does the exact opposite of what you would normally expect it to do.

MARKETING DIRECTOR, GOLD-MINING COMPANY

113

There has been a dramatic shift in our industry towards greater uncertainty. The impact of China and India, especially if they start dumping products, the upsurge in popularity of generics and the regulatory behaviour of governments are all new ingredients in the broth. The result could damage our health!

CEO, GLOBAL HEALTHCARE COMPANY

In the legal industry, the ability to retain talent has become a key uncertainty, especially in light of the new rule of the game in South Africa – black economic empowerment. Black lawyers are in huge demand from all quarters. SENIOR PARTNER, LEADING LAW FIRM

Our competitiveness in the future has become our greatest uncertainty. New prohibitive regulation, shifting market perception and counterfeit cigarette sales in some of our markets all feed into our future ability to compete.

CFO, LEADING INTERNATIONAL TOBACCO COMPANY –
EUROPEAN END-MARKET

Our key uncertainty revolves around the tactics which our biggest competitor in the US will employ to reduce our market share. They go beyond the reasonable. MANAGER, GLOBAL BREWING COMPANY

We've discovered all the 'big easies' – easy to find, easy to mine, easy to treat deposits. Now we're into the 'big toughies' – tough ore bodies in tough countries. It's a rule of the game that you can't move an ore body, so any ore body has associated with it all the uncertainties that go with the country in which it is located.

CEO, GLOBAL MINING COMPANY

The future role of synthetic diamonds is a key uncertainty in my business. Will they become the equivalent of cultured pearls and start displacing natural gems? Nobody knows.

OWNER, DIAMOND JEWELLERY MANUFACTURER

When we enter the 21st century in ten years' time, fundamental Islam will be the definitive uncertainty facing the West. The extent of its influence and ultimate consequences are unknown. Should the spreading of an idea turn into a war of beliefs, a nuclear jihad *is possible.*   MIDDLE EASTERN EXPERT, GLOBAL SCENARIO SESSION, SEPTEMBER 1990

In June 2001, when you published an open letter to George Bush citing a massive terrorist strike on a Western city as his primary threat, why was nobody in the security agencies listening to you? I know you were referring to nukes, but you were spot on in high-lighting the enhanced capability of international terrorist organisa-tions to hit the West on Western soil. I guess that's what the role of scenario planners is – to shake people's trees and rid them of deadly misperceptions. After all, there was the tip-off (which was ignored at the time) of Arabs learning to take off but not land at one American flying school. You'd have provided a new slant to this information which might have resulted in it being processed differently.

DEFENCE INDUSTRY ANALYST

In terms of sustainable development and preserving the global envi-ronment, the key uncertainty is not so much the world's total popu-lation growth but rather how many more people are going to enjoy an American lifestyle now that China and India are experiencing phenomenal economic growth. At present the figure is 900 million out of 6.5 billion; but the number could easily double in the next ten years.   CLIMATE-CHANGE EXPERT, SCENARIO SESSION, LONDON

We have six major uncertainties that could derail the Chinese game. The first is an American recession because we export so much to America. The second is a general rise in international terrorism and turmoil which could disrupt our supply lines and marketing chan-nels. The third is a growing scarcity of raw materials and rising commodity prices created by our own growth in demand as well as

India's. The fourth is increasing social unrest in China should the economy start slowing down. The fifth is the rate of environmental degradation in China itself limiting our prospects, and the sixth is global warming which would necessitate a movement away from the one resource we have – coal.   CHINESE STRATEGIST, BEIJING

A bubble is only a bubble when it is no longer a bubble. Otherwise it is a trend. Such is the uncertainty that always plagues my game.
PARTNER, STOCKBROKING FIRM

If a change in the jet stream caused by global warming was responsible for the recent flooding in England, the unprecedented could become precedented or, in your terminology, a wild card could turn into a rule of the game. Think of the consequences for households in the absence of enhanced flood barriers. We would become the 'Isle of Mud'.   OFFICIAL, ENVIRONMENTAL AGENCY, UK

As America's gambling capital, uncertainty is embedded in our way of life. But if the summers here get any hotter, the tourists will go elsewhere. And that, my friend, is the end of the game.
DELEGATE, TRAVEL CONFERENCE, LAS VEGAS

I've never attended a strategy session where the 'black swan' which lurks in the shadow of the rushes has been so convincingly revealed. By black swan I mean the dark future – full of slit-wrist uncertainties – that can capture you unawares and take you down. Not that I've got anything against the white swans swimming gracefully down the centre of the river. It's just that we all see them coming, because it's how we want the future to pan out.
SITE SUPERVISOR, CONSTRUCTION COMPANY

Life is so uncertain here, I constantly feel like an impala at the waterhole.
PARTICIPANT, CRIME-PREVENTION WORKSHOP, JOHANNESBURG

9 Scenarios: On your gameboard, what are the possible scenarios and where would you position yourself in relation to them now?

I realised that it was not by wisdom that poets write their poetry,
but by a kind of nature or inspiration, such as you find in
seers and prophets; for these also say many beautiful things,
but do not know anything of what they say.
SOCRATES, as quoted by Plato in *Apology*

When replying to the fox's question as to where his destiny would lead him, Socrates responded: "That depends on the outcome of the trial. I could be found not guilty of any crime and continue to debate issues that intrigue me. I could spend the rest of my life in prison. I could be put to death. Three scenarios for which there will be one outcome, but I must be prepared for all three."

Every game we play, whether in life or business, will more than likely have a potential set of different outcomes. These possible outcomes are based on the key uncertainties that play into the game we are in. We call these outcomes 'scenarios', and, in keeping with the metaphor of the game, these scenarios interconnect to form a scenario gameboard. At any time and point in the game we are positioned somewhere on the gameboard, specifically in one of the scenarios. Depending on the external forces that drive the game and on how we choose to play the game, we can move on the gameboard to where we want to be; maintain our position; or, if we allow it, be moved by other players or forces to a less desirable position. Scenarios offer multiple pathways to the future – both good and bad.

Instead of 'outcomes', scenarios are also often defined as different 'plausible future environments'. For example, when Socrates questioned the fox about his future destiny line, and what possibilities and consequences that destiny line might present, the fox replied: "My possibilities are to take my wife and travel north, south, east or west after this conversation. Each path will contain its own string of events and consequences, which will become part of my destiny line." The fox was simply alluding to a set of scenarios that could play out as a result of his interaction with other animals (particularly those that represented a threat) as well as the state of the forest around him. This interplay could still lead the fox to a complex array of possible outcomes, or plausible future environments. For instance, he could start by 'zigging' to the north and then 'zagging' back south if a river blocked his progress.

The Eyes and Ears

For us, of course, given the intense convolution of human emotions and patterns of decision-making, the complexity of outcomes is magnified, and cannot be simplified or ignored, as is often the case in traditional strategy development where a strategy is established, a course is plotted, tracks are laid and the command given to move forward. Ordinary life is anything but rational in the sense of everyday events and actions being propelled by pure reason. Passion is an element of most scenarios, whether we're talking nations, companies or individuals. It takes more than deduction to figure out the possibilities in a non-Platonic world. Moreover, because every scenario is shaped by the interplay between the players, as well as between the players and the environment, the potential for change is high. Such an interplay demands that an examination of oneself and the environment remains an ongoing exercise. We believe this can be achieved by diligently questioning assumptions and debating issues through our conversation model, and referring back to it at any time.

Scenarios help to depict what future environments will look

like, as well as define the capabilities required in order to succeed in any scenario. That's where you hold the mirror up to yourself to see if you do indeed possess those capabilities – and, if not, what you are going to do about it. Scenarios are a crucial tool in the decision-making process in that they help set out the best options for a successful course into the future in the face of significant uncertainty. This may explain why scenarios should be the core of any strategic conversation. They help crystallise the group's strategic thinking and, more often than not, provide the group with an 'aha' moment that acts as an accelerant to the pace and direction of the strategic thinking. Scenarios often allow people to *re-perceive* the future and re-contextualise it, rather than just fixate on a part of it as a predetermined focus point, which is the trend in general strategic thinking. Scenarios provide not only a clearer definition as to where we would like to be in a future state, but also an insight into the paths we do *not* want to follow because the outcome will turn out to be negative for us.

Building and developing scenarios is not an exact science. They are instead a way of tapping into and developing our more intuitive and creative thinking, which is then manifested through the logic and plausibility of each scenario. In essence, scenarios open our thinking and provide us with a window of insight into our future (and into ourselves); and with insight comes clarity of choice. Because we tend to view things through a lens determined by our own DNA, different people have different perceptions of an event. The point of scenarios is to provide a shared window of insight and allow different people to debate the world as it really is – in a more transparent framework – instead of talking past each other as a result of perceiving the world through their individual lenses. Ultimately, a decision will also be enhanced by the fact that scenarios provide a powerful context for our choice, since we never play a game alone or out of the context created by our environment.

Hence, in a group situation, it is wise to form a consensus on which scenario is in play before deciding about the action to be taken. You may still be collectively wrong, but at least you will have been consistent.

Through constant questioning, Socratic dialogue allows us to construct the logic of a scenario via the unveiling of the interplay between cause and effect: if this were to happen, what would be the result and how would the other players react? As already mentioned, the power of doing this also builds a refined awareness of both our capabilities and the environment within which we operate. This is a skill that, as individuals and organisations, we require if we are to observe and anticipate changes, synthesise information around us and give it meaning. The scenarios may never play out in the exact form in which they were constructed, but the very process of constructing the scenarios provides an awareness of our environment that would otherwise have been missed through standard planning techniques. Consequently, this awareness becomes an in-built quality of the organisation, giving it eyes and ears it never had before. Perceptions of new data can be converted into knowledge, i.e. meaningful information in context, at a faster rate with a scenario gameboard than without it.

Finally, at the risk of overplaying the importance of their construction in our strategic thinking process, scenarios also help us develop longer-term perspectives. This is an essential tool for strategy, and yet something that is often glossed over because, naturally, human thinking is more comfortable in the short-term arena. This means that when most organisations are developing strategies for the future (the next 5-10 years), their thinking more often than not remains in the current reality, with short-term actions generally being the desired outcomes. This can lead to a blurred big picture of the 'what's it all about?' kind – or, as one Enron employee put it, "why?". Confusion reigns within the company as management run around the playing field issuing instructions amounting to short-term tactics. Meanwhile the team has no clarity as to where the goalposts are positioned! By using scenarios, however, the long-term purpose of the business can be articulated in a positive story, which can then be cascaded throughout the organisation and serve as a motivational tool.

The Scenario Gameboard

A common misapprehension is that, for scenarios to be effective, they need to be highly detailed and go through a process of many iterations involving lots of workshops. This is not true. If scenarios are overcomplicated, they can lose their appeal and thus their usefulness. What must be done is to assure a degree of differentiation between the scenarios such that each of them registers clearly in the minds of the participants. The last thing you want is someone saying: "I can't see the difference between your first and your third scenarios." When facilitating strategic conversations, we therefore continue with the game analogy and design a one-page *scenario gameboard* – like any other gameboard such as that used in Monopoly. It features catchy and meaningful names that have been suggested and embraced by the participants. These gameboards then become platforms for understanding the future. Obviously, for each scenario displayed on the gameboard, a text or a series of bullet points accompanies it.

Each gameboard is developed by considering a list of principal variables that can affect the topic chosen for the scenarios, be it the future possibilities for the world economy, for the industry you're in, or for your organisation. The two pivotal uncertainties that will have the most influence on the game, or impact on the organisation, are then selected. It is these two pivotal uncertainties that, represented as intersecting axes, create the framework for the gameboard: a 2 x 2 matrix containing four scenarios, namely a best-case scenario, a worst-case scenario and two intermediate scenarios. In game parlance, these would respectively be called a 'win' scenario, a 'loss' scenario and two 'draw' scenarios. Developing worst-case (or loss) scenarios is an essential part of understanding the future, as it provides a greater consciousness of the signs indicating impending danger. There is also as much strategic insight to be gained in discussing ways of steering the organisation away from worst-case scenarios as there is in pointing the helm towards the desirable one.

The variables for constructing a gameboard may both be external, i.e. outside of the control of the organisation (such as that for the global geopolitical or national economic game); or they may consist of one largely outside of and one largely inside the control of the organisation, e.g. having the state of the market as the horizontal axis and the competitiveness of the organisation – relative to its competitors – as the vertical axis. This is possibly the most popular matrix we have used for businesses. There is an alternative business gameboard, where an organisation can plot a possible change in strategic direction on one axis and competitiveness on the other, in which case both axes are pretty much within its control. This gameboard is particularly useful when a change in strategic direction is contemplated. Whichever model of gameboard is used, as long as the variables represent the parameters by which you want to measure the environment or yourself or both, you'll have a lot of fun pinpointing your current position on the board. By considering two gameboards – the international economic and specific business ones – the interdependencies and connectedness between the two provide a strong overall picture of the whole game. It always does an organisation good to put its own strategic path within the context of the bigger game.

To illustrate the method of construction of these different

models of gameboards, we have developed three different examples: an international, a national and a business gameboard.

The Global Gameboard

The best example we can give of the first type of matrix (where both variables are external) is the one we are currently using to demonstrate the different possibilities for the future state of the world, politically and economically. The vertical axis relates to whether globalisation continues to be the grand, unifying force it is, or whether the world enters an era of fragmentation driven by national and religious rivalries. The horizontal axis is simply based on the global economic growth rate and whether (on the right) it can be sustained at over 5 per cent per annum; or whether (on the left) it falls back into the zero to 3 per cent range. The middle part of the gameboard represents a rate somewhere between 3 and 5 per cent.

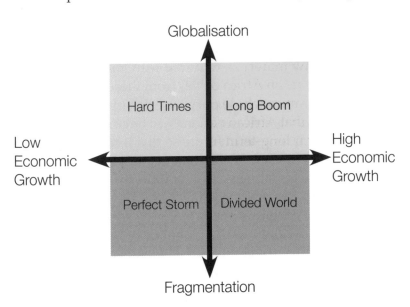

Going clockwise from the top right, we have the following scenarios:

Long Boom

The world was located in this scenario for most of the 1990s, and remained so in the opening years of the new century. The *Long Boom* is driven by the conversion of most countries to free-market economics and the spectacular rise of China and India. The party continues, with inflation and interest rates remaining low, the Chinese and Indian economies continuing to defy gravity and stock markets continuing to boom. The world still has conflict zones, but the impact of these is completely overridden by the unstoppable force of globalisation. One day either global warming, a growing scarcity of raw materials, the latter causing a general rise in inflation rates, or a new global health epidemic could moderate the boom.

A *Long Boom* scenario envisages the centre of gravity of the world economy moving East, meaning that Western institutions like the IMF and World Bank will have to revise their mode of operation. The scenario also brings other players onto the global playing field, such as Africa. African countries have many of the raw materials required for China and India's growth. The focus on Africa comes from these two countries as well as companies whose purpose is to supply them. This in turn implies that African nations will have more influence to negotiate their long-term future so that it comes to pass in a sustainable manner. Nevertheless, they need to build the necessary negotiating skills to compel the counterparties to add value to the raw materials *before* they leave the national borders. With this one proviso, *African Sunrise* – the continent's equivalent to the global *Long Boom* scenario – becomes a distinct possibility. An incidental consequence of the *Long Boom* is that the G8 will eventually become the G10 with the addition of China and India as new members.

Divided World

The world develops into a more hostile place as regional conflicts intensify and trading spats/cases of protectionism multiply. In this scenario, the anti-globalisation lobby grows stronger while an increasing number of countries reject the 'Washington consensus', revert to old-style Socialist policies (some in South America) and become more nationalistic about the resources they possess (Russia). Nevertheless, just as no terrorist incident or war in the recent past has been a show stopper (not even 9/11), the global economy shrugs off all these problems because of the sheer momentum caused by the two most populous nations on earth simultaneously going through an industrial revolution. Whereas in the *Long Boom* companies can invest virtually anywhere in the world because the tide is rising everywhere, they have to be more circumspect in *Divided World* because of the emergence of more 'failed states'.

Perfect Storm

As the name suggests, this scenario represents a confluence of negative events in both the political and economic arenas, which could lead to a huge change in the fortunes of the world. It is a reprise of the 'roaring' 1920s, which was followed by the depression of the 1930s and the rise of Nazi Germany. The party ends just as spectacularly – only the script and the actors are different. Potential triggers could be nuclear terrorism in a Western city, a major war between Iran and Israel/the West over its nuclear programme, a new Cold War as Russia reverts to authoritarianism, or a financial meltdown in China followed by widespread unrest. Recovery from this scenario proves to be agonisingly slow, as business confidence has to be rebuilt from scratch. Remember that leading Wall Street stocks only recovered their peak 1929 value over 25 years later (having shed 89 per cent by 1932). It was a 'long drop'!

This is a scenario of conventional global recession, probably initiated by a US economic downturn and the knock-on effect it has on the other economies. India and China are not spared, as the interdependencies created by globalisation and international trade turn against them. Asset prices (property and equities), the improvement of which has over recent years allowed consumers to borrow more to spend, suddenly reverse. The downward spiral is reinforced when commodity prices plummet, except for gold that does well in light of the uncertainties around paper currencies and paper assets. Eventually the blood-letting ends, green shoots start springing up in the burnt landscape and a recovery gets under way, which returns the world to the top right-hand quadrant. The length of the recession is relatively short, i.e. it is more like a 'V' than a 'U', but the depth of the 'V' is unknown. The crucial difference between *Hard Times* and *Perfect Storm* is that globalisation remains intact in the former scenario, while it is seriously compromised by political and military events in the latter one. The rebound in the second case therefore takes much longer.

These descriptions or 'short stories' paint a brief picture of the suite of scenarios, and allude to their different characteristics. As we've already intimated, the differences can also be expressed in a series of bullet points. However, it must be remembered that the object of interest of the scenarios – in this case the world economy – is not static. Every news bulletin means a dynamic reappraisal of the situation as events unfold; and because the name of the game in business is to acquire knowledge and truth faster than your competitor, any business that notices a shift in the commercial environment before its competitors do will always have the upper hand. The secret is to know what signs, or leading indicators, to look for that herald a shift in the game, or more fundamentally announce that you are about to cross into a different part of the game-board (i.e. enter a new scenario). We have registered some of the indicators in the narrative of our international scenarios.

Equally important is to work out in advance what the consequences of the new scenarios are for your strategy, so you can immediately exercise other options if need be. Moreover, over time the scenarios themselves will lose relevancy if they are not updated. So even the gameboard is dynamic!

National Gameboard

For a country, the two pivotal uncertainties are its competitiveness on the global playing field as well as, from an internal perspective, the state of its society, i.e. whether it is characterised by harmony or conflict.

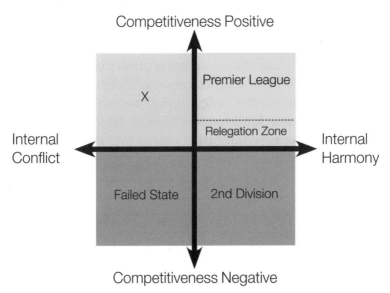

You will note that the top left-hand quadrant of the gameboard has been marked with an 'X'. It signifies that we rule out this scenario altogether on the grounds that it is not sustainable.

A country cannot be riven by internal conflict and still be competitive. Hence, there remain three scenarios and again we start in the upper right-hand corner:

Premier League

To be in the *Premier League* scenario, a country should enjoy a high level of social harmony and act as a cohesive team. The economy is 'inclusive', with a low unemployment rate and acceptable income differences between the classes. At the same time, the country is competitive because it possesses the attributes of a 'winning nation' which include quality education; a strong working ethic; a high savings rate and an adequate infrastructure to cope with economic expansion. It positions itself as an export-oriented global player by exploiting its strengths to differentiate itself from other nations. It develops a dual-logic economy where world-class global businesses combine with a thriving small business sector to create synergies between the two. Tax rates are competitive, the environment for foreign direct investment is attractive and above all government is efficient (particularly regarding health services).

Countries fall into the 'Relegation Zone' when they decline in competitiveness for whatever reason. This is a dangerous area to be in, because relegation means that the country will no longer enjoy the privileges of being a member of the top league – and it's very hard to get back into it. The *Long Boom* scenario has conferred Premier League status on quite a few developing countries – particularly resource-rich ones – that have taken advantage of the positive economic climate.

2nd Division

This scenario is for countries that are poor but peaceful. They remain *2nd Division* players either because they have no ambition to move up to the *Premier League*, or they are quite bereft of mineral resources, or nature is harsh in terms of climate or soil. But they get by and, the human spirit being what it is, the people lead relatively contented lives. The *2nd Division* also contains ex-Premier League nations that once were rich but whose income per head has declined for any number of reasons including bad leadership. They don't wield much influence in global affairs and seldom obtain anything prestigious like a seat on the UN Security Council. They may even possess some of the attributes of a 'winning nation', but somehow they simply cannot get their entire act together.

Failed State

This scenario is characterised by high levels of unemployment, gross inequality of income and appalling human rights abuse including routine torture. 'Government' is either a malevolent dictator living in a palace among the ruins of the country around him, where conflict is kept in check through intimidation; or it is a shifting alliance of warlords, each with a private army or militia. Here, conflict can range from a low-intensity to high-intensity civil war, depending on whether the informal coalitions are holding together or falling apart. Those with the means and skills in a *Failed State* are the first to emigrate, taking their capital with them. Thereafter, ordinary citizens become refugees, fleeing for their lives when the situation becomes really desperate.

We have purposefully omitted to put names of countries into any of the three scenarios because we want you, the reader, to decide where you would allocate your own country, and other countries as well. Moreover, the national gameboard shouldn't be examined without reference to the international gameboard. For example, should there be a global move from a *Long Boom* towards a *Hard Times* or *Perfect Storm* scenario, it is quite possible for a country that is in the 'Relegation Zone' of the *Premier League* to slip into the *2nd Division* scenario, with the chance of then sliding into a *Failed State* if conditions appreciably worsen. The converse is also true: should the world remain in a *Long Boom,* the consequential flourishing of international trade could help some countries that are in the *2nd Division* to be promoted into the *Premier League* (obviously because they have succeeded in developing a comparative advantage in specific areas which are in demand).

The Business Gameboard

This is the scenario gameboard that in our facilitations has proven the most popular among companies. If you really concentrate on what drives a company's long-term profitability, it boils down to two factors: the attractiveness of the game that it chooses to play and its competitiveness in that game. Let's use a sports analogy to buttress this point. If you are the reigning world champion at squash, you will never earn a vast amount of money since it does not draw mass audiences. Hence, from a financial point of view, it is not an attractive game. In contrast, if you are the world's premier golfer or Formula One driver, you will earn a fortune. Even if you are past your best and declining in competitiveness, you will still earn a lot of money. A squash player will earn nothing!

The same principles carry through to business. This is why we've chosen the horizontal axis of the business gameboard to denote the state of the market in which the company is selling its goods and/or services, and the vertical axis its competitiveness in the market. Both areas have features which are within and beyond the control of the company. Taking the market axis first, what is inside a company's control is to choose which market, or if it has a variety of business units which markets, it should be in. Clearly, once a market has been chosen, there are plenty of factors beyond the company's control, such as the general level of demand for the product; whether it is outstripping supply or whether the market is constantly saturated because of the number of other suppliers of an identical or similar product; the availability of substitutes in the event of price increases the public don't like; the possibility of product obsolescence due to technical advances; and the stability/economic growth of the countries in which the revenues are being derived. On top of this is the general state of the global economy and whether it is in a boom or a recession.

Relative competitiveness, on the other hand, depends on how effectively the company is being managed in areas such as cost containment and service delivery (inside its control), but also on the relative performance of existing competitors, the advent of new competition and the movement of currency exchange rates which may affect its ranking in the international cost league (all outside of its control).

In considering these two axes, some executive teams like to keep their definition fairly general and intuitive, while others unpack the meaning using key performance indicators.

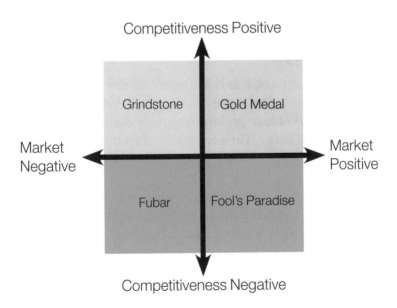

One of the reasons for the popularity of this gameboard is the effectiveness of the names in projecting the image of the scenarios. Contrary to the other two gameboards, we normally start with the bottom left quadrant, move to the bottom right, then top left and finally top right. This means that the scenarios are presented in ascending order of desirability.

Fubar

This is obviously the worst-case scenario, where your competitiveness is declining in a poor market. The stark reality is that you're uncompetitive in an unattractive game. Incidentally, the name of this scenario first arose during a strategy session one of us was facilitating for a leading South African company. Those familiar with military slang will know that *Fubar* is an acronym for something a little more desperate than simply 'mucked up beyond all recognition'! Suffice it to say that the scenario is now well established in the oral tradition of the company. No company wants to be in this scenario, because it is the last stage before bankruptcy and death. Best to change the game or conduct major surgery.

Fool's Paradise

As the name suggests, this is a nonsustainable position where all the company's faults are covered by a booming market. Should the market turn and the company does nothing, it will go directly into *Fubar*. Time to jack up the efficiencies.

Grindstone

We've all been here – a scenario where you put your nose to the grindstone and grind out better efficiencies than your competitors in a hostile market. Not a bad place to be since an improvement in the market can put you in *Gold Medal* territory. It's also a quadrant where you can launch a takeover bid for a competitor because the tough market makes its shares cheap. Inevitably, some of your product range or business units may lie in this quadrant and will continue to do so. But they are an essential part of your product offering, so you have to live with the 'grind'.

Gold Medal

This is where you want to be. Your competitiveness is growing in an attractive market. As the title suggests, you're winning the game. The challenge is to maintain your competitive streak despite being showered with success. However, if you become complacent and take your foot off the pedal you could slip into *Fool's Paradise*. The big issue is whether you're putting enough resources behind the products or businesses that belong to you and are in *Gold Medal* territory.

During the conversation around the scenarios, the questions to ask are: where is the company on the gameboard at the moment, and where have you come from during, say, the last five years? But the fun really starts when you drill down and ask where each of the business units should be positioned and, even further down, where each of the products resides. The gameboard gives you a very good pictorial feel of your portfolio of businesses and products and immediately suggests strategies for each of them.

Other sub-questions that may be asked include:

- Where would you place each of your major competitors on the gameboard?
- Do you think that your business or product mix should change as a result of reviewing the gameboard?
- How do the international and national gameboard scenarios impact on your positioning on the business gameboard?
- Do you have any second thoughts on the scope of the

business that you discussed earlier as a result of the insights gained from the gameboard?

Of course, a company must feel absolutely free to design its own business gameboard with its own variables, should it wish to do so. Moreover, NGOs, for example, use different parameters such as relevance of service offering and financial sustainability as the two key parameters in constructing the board. But whatever you do, please remember to come up with intriguing names for the scenarios – ones that the team are unlikely to forget. A certain amount of humour and irreverence also comes in handy. It's a great way to get across serious themes in a non-threatening way and keep the creative juices flowing.

Here are some of the memorable comments made during the scenario section of the debate (and again we've listed a considerable number for illustration):

When considering our position as a country on the global playing field, we should construct scenarios using GDP per capita in US dollars as one axis and exports as a percentage of GDP as our other axis. Three scenarios come to mind. We have a 'Grounded' scenario with low GDP per capita and a low export percentage. Like an aircraft stranded on the runway through mechanical problems, the country goes nowhere. The second scenario is 'Take Off', where a country uses its strengths – which in our case include our minerals – to raise the export percentage to a point where the economy starts rolling. The third scenario, which we all want to be in, is 'Flying High', with high GDP per capita, high exports, an attractive environment for foreign direct investment and an efficient government. Right now, we are grounded, but the turnaround time for take-off is shorter than people think.

PARTICIPANT, SCENARIO WORKSHOP ON ZIMBABWE

Our scenarios are 'Survivor' where, despite increasing regulation, we manage to grow our revenue by increasing cigarette sales in Third World markets; 'Crime and Punishment', where excessive regulation starts driving us out of business; 'Barbarians at the Gate', where we get taken over; and 'Brave New World', where we seriously promote nonsmoking nicotine products as part of our product range. Not only are the latter less harmful, but people will be able to consume these products in public places while enjoying a smoke at home. EXECUTIVE, GLOBAL TOBACCO COMPANY, UK

We have just won the largest number of global awards that an advertising agency could win. I guess that would put us in the 'Gold Medal' scenario. Is that a good thing? Well, it scares me in that we now have to try and maintain our position. This will require a review of our strategy and a new set of tactics in light of changing trends in the market. EXECUTIVE, GLOBAL ADVERTISING AGENCY

As a member of the nonferrous metals industry in Europe, a very likely scenario is high global economic growth, but a low ability on our side to compete. An appropriate name for this scenario is 'Chinese Water Torture'.
PARTICIPANT, EUROMETAUX SCENARIO WORKSHOP

Our best-case scenario has been cascaded throughout our organisation and is now deeply embedded in all of our actions and decisions. It is called 'Deep Green'.
SENIOR EXECUTIVE, MAJOR BANKING GROUP

Finding names for our scenarios helped us to build a strong understanding of the strategic options available to us. We used the weather as our theme and called the scenarios 'African Sky Blue', 'Scattered Thundershowers', 'Gale Force' and 'Perfect Storm'. They helped us to decide whether or not to split our auditing business from our consulting side. SENIOR PARTNER, LEADING ACCOUNTING FIRM

Four scenarios can play out in the gold market:

- 'Bull Run', where growth in jewellery demand, especially from China and India, takes place against a background of a scarcity of new mines. This combination sees the gold price hitting $1 000 an ounce;
- 'Mellow Yellow', where new demand is balanced by new supply and the price hovers between $500 and $800;
- 'Big Dipper', where a world traumatised by an escalation in terror speculates on gold and the price fluctuates between $400 and $900; and
- 'Golden Bear', where some major new gold field is found, investment demand falls because of continuing low rates of inflation and the price slumps to between $300 and $500.

Take your pick!   CEO, GOLD-MINING COMPANY

The wine industry is definitely in the 'Grindstone' scenario because of the wine lake across the world. In order to move towards 'Gold Medal', we will need to differentiate ourselves with a wine in the ultra-premium category.

MARKETING DIRECTOR, INTERNATIONAL WINE MAKER

Post 2012, when the Kyoto agreement comes to an end, four policy scenarios on climate change are possible, depending on the level of political will and degree of co-operation between nations. The worst is 'Dirty Dancing', where everybody goes their own way with no restraints on carbon emissions. Slightly better is 'Different Dances', where at least some nations seek to limit their emissions in an uncoordinated way. 'Dances with Wolves' is where a new agreement is achieved but several parties immediately cheat on it. The best-case scenario is 'Strictly Ballroom', where all countries fall into step and waltz together under a new dispensation. But will they, given the level of rivalry and antagonism that exists in the world today? We'll have to wait and see.

PARTICIPANT, CLIMATE-CHANGE WORKSHOP, LONDON

*Essentially, there are two scenarios for China. The positive one,
'Harmonious World', is where China achieves a significant level of
harmony on three levels:*

- *harmony between the rural poor and the urban elite inside
  China, by putting greater emphasis on rural development and
  at the same time building new cities to take people off the land
  into higher-paying urban jobs;*
- *harmony between man and nature by re-orienting the economy from heavy industry into services and by improving energy
  efficiencies; and*
- *harmony between China and the rest of the world by ensuring that other countries prosper as a result of China's success
  and China is seen as a beneficial force in world affairs.*

*The negative scenario for China is 'Polarising World', where exog-
enous shocks to its economy – either through an escalation in the
war of terror, increasing protectionism by European countries or a
recession in the US – cause economic growth to fall by at least five
percentage points. This could cause widespread social upheaval in
China as people's expectations are no longer met, which in turn
could mean a new clique in the Communist Party emerging to take
over the reins of power.*　　　　CHINESE ACADEMIC, BEIJING

*Australia could experience two scenarios: 'On Golden Pond', where
the country gradually subsides into an old-world economy, but the
decline is quite graceful; and 'Matilda Changes Step', where a whole
raft of new industries are created to replace the resource sector.*

　　　PARTICIPANT, SCENARIO WORKSHOP ON AUSTRALIA

*Our current reality in Cape Town has been described in a scenario-
planning exercise as 'Southern Comfort'. This is something akin to
the early days of the south-eastern states of America, where the few
live in grand style and great comfort, while the many struggle to
eke out a living and suffer great hardship, oblivious to the natural
beauty that surrounds them.*　　　CEO, ACCELERATE CAPE TOWN

We have decided to use key performance indicators to locate our position on your business gameboard. For competitiveness, we are in the top half of your chart if we hold the No. 1 or No. 2 ranking in the national survey of asset managers. That also applies to the funds under our supervision. We are on the line if we are No. 3 and, anything lower than that, we are below the line. For the market, the right-hand side of the gameboard represents a bull market for the period under review, and the left-hand side a bear market. Simple! And we'll do a scattergram on your gameboard of all the funds we manage to get a feel for who's who in the zoo when it comes to bonus time. CEO, LEADING ASSET-MANAGEMENT COMPANY

We are entering a new era for the mining industry and there are four scenarios depending on whether or not demand will continue to outstrip supply, and whether or not over time Eastern mining companies will challenge the might of Western mining companies. The first scenario, which we are in at the moment, is 'Rational Exuberance', where the mining boom continues and the existing multinationals hold sway and prosper. If the market reverts to normal, we will be back to 'Classical Rules', where the costs of the marginal producer determine the commodity price. High-grade mines will still make plenty of money. If the centre of gravity of the mining industry moves East, the scenario changes to 'Chinese Chess' because of the number of new Chinese, Indian and Russian mining companies entering the market with lots of deals being done. The last scenario is 'Hard Ball', where the negotiations turn nasty because the market goes flat just as all these new players have entered it. They battle for business on their own terms.

EXECUTIVE, GLOBAL MINING COMPANY

With the level of multitasking in this organisation, the downside scenario is 'Empty Wheels'. It's when the hamsters quit because they're so exhausted! STAFF MEMBER, LEADING BUSINESS SCHOOL

PLAYING THE GAME

10 SWOT: What are your strengths and weaknesses as a player; and what are the opportunities and threats offered by the game?

Whenever, therefore, people are deceived and form opinions wide of the truth, it is clear that the error has slid into their minds through the medium of certain resemblances to that truth.
SOCRATES, as quoted by Plato in *Phaedrus*

SWOT? So what?

We've heard that comment a number of times from people who have worked through a SWOT exercise at their organisation's annual strategy session. SWOT is a well-known process in business strategy and, being quite straightforward, its popularity up till now has been relatively assured. The basic assumption is that a quick whiz through an organisation's strengths, weaknesses, opportunities and threats will somehow throw out deep insights. Opinions as to the next step forward are then drawn from the analysis in the belief that the result will contribute towards moving the organisation in the correct strategic direction.

Sometimes it does, sometimes it doesn't. But the limitation of a SWOT analysis lies in the way it is normally done as an isolated exercise and repeated over and over again – until people suffer from SWOT fatigue. Thereafter, it's a case of going through the motions with little follow-through, other than someone being allocated the task of turning it into a nice graphic for the strategic document. It is amazing how often participants in our sessions wheel out the previous year's SWOT analysis without conviction or enthusiasm. They expect nothing from a revisit. Consequently, unless SWOT is given its proper place in the strategic conversation, its value as a tool will continue to decline in the 'appreciation stakes'.

A Lesson in DIY

We believe that we have discovered the right place. SWOT should form the link between *defining* the game and *playing* the game. If a strategic conversation was, say, a DIY (do-it-yourself) task, defining the game would be ascertaining what had to be done, playing the game would be doing it, and SWOT would be examining the tools you had at your disposal and what tools might still be needed. In the world of DIY, running through your list of tools *before* you have established the nature of the job to be done would not be particularly helpful. In a similar vein, doing a SWOT exercise on its own is pretty pointless, whereas doing it as part of a strategic conversation – after establishing the nature of the game – immediately places your abilities in context and provides a valuable reference point for what is still required. In other words, SWOT becomes a powerful tool for probing your skills gap.

Furthermore, anticipating the dynamic changes in a game is only halfway to winning it. Not great odds at 50/50! It is often said that knowing is one thing; doing is another. One of our greatest weaknesses as humans lies in our limited ability to bridge that knowing-doing gap. Performing a SWOT analysis at this stage of the strategic conversation provides that bridge between knowing the game and playing the game. In essence, a SWOT analysis provides the most realistic assessment of your profile and situation before you start investigating the strategic choices and tactics in the game.

In the conversation between Socrates and the fox, Socrates – after hearing the fox's story – was determined that they both should have some measure of insight into its practical implications. He asked the fox: "What are we going to take away from our conversation and do? For as we both know, actions speak more loudly than words." The fox explained that his whole destiny line to that point had involved a growing understanding of his strengths and weaknesses; and that unless they tackled the question of their strengths, weaknesses and immediate opportunities and threats, any talk of possible action would be purely academic. In the fox's words: "What you are does not determine what you will be or what you can be, but it sure as hell has an influence over your next move."

Perhaps we should examine more closely how the fox's interpretation of strengths, weaknesses, opportunities and threats applies in the milieu of commerce. Strengths and weaknesses are inner dimensions that relate, among other things, to the quality of leadership at the top; the existing competencies and prevailing ethos among employees; the financial resources at the organisation's disposal and even its business model, brand and internal structure. Opportunities and threats are external dimensions – lying outside of the office walls – and relate more to changes in the rules of the game as well as to the uncertainties associated with the external environment. However, as we have stressed on several occasions in this book, while the appearance of an opportunity or threat may lie outside of an organisation's control, the seizing of the opportunity or response to the threat is definitely within the remit of management.

The Gameboard Connection

The last point brings to mind the gameboard of the previous chapter. For, consider this: your strengths and weaknesses (and how you modify them) move you up or down the competitiveness axis; whereas opportunities and threats (and your response to them) move you left or right depending on how they influence the attractiveness of the game. It all ties in and gives the SWOT analysis the logical foundation it lacks when done as a stand-alone exercise. But don't forget that the definition of competitiveness can change as the game changes.

Different strengths will make you competitive at different times. For example, one small process-control company told us that they used to rely on developing long-term relationships with clients to win contracts. It was their strength. Now with higher staff turnover in client companies, personal contacts are a thing of the past. Their bids are handled by faceless tender committees who only look at price and not at the quality of service which accompanies the installation of the equipment. Their strength has been effectively neutralised.

By contrast, in another arena altogether, war games have also changed to such an extent that different capabilities are required to be a first-rate military force. As Major General Les Rudman of the South African National Defence Force puts it: "The South African Army needs a force that is able to wage both war and peace at the same time." You need a 'big-stick' warrior force backed up by a 'baton-stick' constabulary force. He quotes Josephus' words in 100 AD: "The Romans are sure of victory. For their exercises are battles without bloodshed and their battles bloody exercises." But in the end the Roman Empire fell apart because all their strengths became weaknesses. They did not recognise the changes in the game – nor did they really care.

In light of the fact that an organisation's SWOT should always be examined within the context of the game, its true value emerges with sub-questions such as the following:

- If you now were to examine the SWOT of your rivals in the game, how do you measure up? Are what you thought were your 'strengths' really so? The answer to this question will very much depend on your points of differentiation from your competitors.
- If events in the commercial environment were to bring about a shift in your position on the business gameboard,

how would you cope in relation to your competitors (bearing in mind your SWOT and theirs)?

■ In what way does your SWOT change in the different quadrants of the international and national scenario gameboards? Does, for example, one of your strengths come to the fore under a particular scenario? Could one of your weaknesses prove potentially destructive in another scenario? How resilient are you to the slings and arrows of global or national misfortune?

■ Is it perhaps time to invest more in the game or get out of it altogether (SWOT is the 'last-chance saloon' to discuss this issue)?

A Different SWOT

A SWOT analysis, as suggested by the fox and modified by us, therefore falls into line with the critical concept that underpins our strategic thinking: the key to success in any game is understanding the interplay between yourself and the environment. Just as the scope of the game must be defined within the context of looking at one's reflection in the 'looking glass', so should a SWOT analysis be a combination of introspection and gazing at the horizon. But SWOT can go beyond merely crystallising your capabilities to play the game and enhancing your powers of perception. It can actually provide a formula for winning the game. This requires a subtle redefinition of SWOT's different components, as follows:

■ **S** for 'Start' – In order to *start* playing the game and be a viable player, you need to know the *strengths* that set you apart. Do you have any distinctive competencies in areas like research and development, one-of-a-kind product design, locking in distribution channels, strong branding or being a low-cost producer? Distinctive competencies are usually a basket of strengths that together are hard to copy. They raise the barrier to entry. Without them you will in all likelihood be a nonstarter, unable to pass 'Go' on the gameboard. These strengths should set you apart from your competitors and, should the game change, be re-examined for their future validity.

- **W** for 'Winning' – When you enter the game it must be done with the end-point of *winning* the game in mind. As in the game of tennis, this often means simply making fewer mistakes and therefore not losing. In golf you don't necessarily scrutinise your game when you win, but you do scrutinise your game if you lose. By identifying and then obviating your *weaknesses,* you can reduce the chances of playing a losing game.
- **O** for 'Outmanoeuvring' – In order to play a game to its fullest and continually maintain a competitive advantage, a player needs to *outmanoeuvre* his or her competitors. Identifying *opportunities* before competitors do will enable you to seize those opportunities first, and then build your organisation's skills around those opportunities.
- **T** for 'Thriving' – Thriving in a game relies on eliminating or, at least, minimising risk, and ensuring that contingency plans are in place for those risks that are out of your control. *Threats* are external risks and should therefore be identified and managed in order to achieve long-term sustainability and viability, i.e. to thrive over the long run in the game. Above all, *thriving* means having fun on and off the court!

SWOT, so what? I think we've managed to show that in the proper context the what becomes 'so, this is your reality check', an invaluable step in strategy design. Furthermore, at this particular stage in our conversation model, SWOT acts as a funnel for all the data which has been amassed in defining the game to be consolidated into a punchy tabulation. Armed with this information, you are ready to enter the next stage of the conversation, that of realistically entertaining the options you have for *playing* the game. SWOT has produced some marvellous comments from participants, which we reproduce below:

Our biggest threat in light of the latest marriage in our industry is that someone else we know follows suit, but we remain a wallflower.

EXECUTIVE, RETAIL BANK

As an island in the Caribbean, our greatest strength is offering an attractive destination for tourists. We also have the added leverage of a reggae culture made famous by Bob Marley – and you can't get a stronger brand than that. However, our biggest threat is on our doorstep: Cuba. It is a beautiful country with many unique characteristics. If it should open up to international tourism, the effects could be devastating for us.

PARTICIPANT, SCENARIO WORKSHOP ON JAMAICA

An opportunity for us is to become another state of the US. On reflection, that would possibly translate into a weakness over time because of the security hassles our tourists would encounter at our airports. PARTICIPANT, SCENARIO WORKSHOP ON JAMAICA

One of our key strengths is our size. We are a highly profitable radio station with a very large listenership firmly concentrated in the highest-earning segment. This has also, strangely enough, been our biggest weakness, because it has brought about complacency and left us with a lack of focus. We're also in an industry where the success of one's product is there for everyone to copy. New competition is therefore a threat that may necessitate a tighter positioning around the competencies that made us great in the first place.

CEO, LEADING SOUTH AFRICAN RADIO STATION

Talent retention (especially young talent) is one of our critical areas of weakness. We recognise loyalty but not specifically talent. We will need to develop performance indicators for this area of human resources. We are also a highly risk-averse company, which in today's world is a weakness. We cannot afford to lag behind our competitors.   EXECUTIVE, LEADING ALCOHOLIC BEVERAGE COMPANY

The 2010 Soccer World Cup will be South Africa's grand opportunity to position itself as a brand in the global market. The spotlight will be that much brighter, as it will be the first time that this – the world's biggest event – will be staged on the African continent. At the same time, this occasion brings with it all measures of threats in the event of non-delivery.
TOP SOUTH AFRICAN BUSINESS EXECUTIVE, WORKSHOP ON 2010

Our principal opportunities and threats lie in our relationship with America. The latter is as good and as bad as it can reasonably be.
PROFESSOR, CENTRAL PARTY SCHOOL, BEIJING

Our opportunity is to capitalise on the expansion of South Africa's two largest ports (Durban and Richards Bay) as well as the new airport. The reason is that we own prime land in the corridor between the two ports and the airport.   PROPERTY DEVELOPER

A fire raging out of control in one of our suburbs is now our biggest threat.   MUNICIPAL CEO, SYDNEY, AUSTRALIA

Copper is our strength. Corruption our weakness.
PARTICIPANT, SCENARIO WORKSHOP ON THE
DEMOCRATIC REPUBLIC OF CONGO, KINSHASA

Our CEO is our strength because he is a legend in our industry and initiates most of our business. But he is also our weakness because of our huge dependency on him (with no clear succession plan).
DIRECTOR, ADVERTISING AGENCY

Despite our success, our only shareholder is about to dispose of our shares because we are considered non-core to their business. The threat is that we don't get on with the new owners.

EXECUTIVE, PRECISION ENGINEERING COMPANY, GERMANY

The big opportunity for us is to hang on to the coat-tails of our clients and follow them into Africa.

CEO, SUPPLIER TO MAJOR RETAIL CHAINS

Our opportunity is to use our brand and expertise to expand our global footprint (or should I say roadprint!), since the market at home has become a zero-sum game.

EXECUTIVE, TARMAC COMPANY, UK

Preservation of the cold chain is fundamental to our business, so the rising frequency of power failures is one of our biggest threats. It will subject our products to greater thermal abuse at the retail level.

EXECUTIVE, GLOBAL FROZEN FOODS COMPANY

Given the shortage of technical skills in South Africa, the opportunity is to provide a 911 service where our electronics engineers act like paramedics. When clients experience equipment breakdowns, our guys will quickly arrive at the scene and sort out the mess – for a fee.

CEO, ELECTRONICS COMPANY

The point you make about looking inwards and outwards certainly applies to me. I taught children in secondary school, and then quite by accident I moved to a primary school. I've never looked back, because the strengths in my character obviously suit the needs of the kids I now teach. Fortuitously, the external world and I have achieved a perfect state of harmony.

PRIMARY SCHOOL TEACHER

11 Options: Within your span of control, what options do you have to improve your current performance and longer-term prospects in the game?

> *The hour of departure has arrived, and we go our ways –*
> *I to die and you to live. Which is better, God only knows.*
> SOCRATES, as quoted by Plato in *Apology*

Having arrived at this point in the conversation, you should have a realistic understanding of the game and its nuances. You have also established a realistic assessment of your own profile and the situation in which you find yourself, and therefore are conscious of how you are faring as a player. This means that when you consider your options, you can do so from a more robust starting point. It also means that options become clearer and easier to flesh out; in fact at this stage the options are often obvious. What still remains something of a challenge is how to convert those options into decisions.

In order to extract the ones of greatest value, options need to be dissected and positioned in the correct perspective. Some options are simple, others more complex in their potential outcomes. For example, the fox asked of Socrates, "'What options do you have?' I've outlined mine, which are pretty simple and relate to the part of the forest I want to sleep in tonight." Socrates explained his options: he could escape before the trial started, but that would damage his legacy; he could reconsider his public stance on the war and the way Athens was governed, but that would also damage his legacy; or he could stand trial and stick to his principles and face possible death. A tortuous array of outcomes indeed!

Sometimes it is a set of options working together that produces the most effective result; at other times a single option can create huge leverage in the game. Whatever their nature, options should as far as possible be played out to their end-point in order to fully understand their consequences, both intended and possibly unintended.

Choosing options relates back to your DNA, and your DNA defines the way you play the game. Of course, good leaders can change the DNA of the organisation they run, but it takes time. Moreover, while business has its mavericks, most of us are risk-averse and err on the more cautious, or conservative, side. This is why so few players really stand out in a game, and why most form the bulk of the pelaton (the main body of cyclists in the *Tour de France*). They breeze along in other people's slipstream. Accordingly, participants in any strategic conversation should preferably be as diverse as possible (within the parameter of being at the correct management level) in order for all the options to be explored effectively.

Strategic and Tactical Options

Options to improve the scope of your game as well as your performance in it broadly fall into two categories that should be considered side by side. The first set draws on your *external* perspective of the game, whereas the second set relates to the *internal* perspective you have of your organisation as a player. The external perspective focuses on the business port-folio – what the product/service offering of the organisation is – and throws light on the most promising direction for the organisation, given the different scenarios. This is pure strat-egy. The internal perspective looks at organisational capability and builds options to help the organisation meet the needs of the game. This constitutes tactics.

Options are therefore classified as either *strategic* or *tactical*. There should be fewer strategic options than tactical options, and these should be debated first in the conversation because they relate back to the scope. Obviously, if the rules of the game have changed drastically or the uncertainties/scenarios offer huge challenges, a significant amount of time may be spent on these options.

Strategic options can be ranked as follows:

- If your SWOT shows that you are a strong player in your current game, you may embark on an *organic-growth* strategy using options that tap into your core competencies, or go for a *stepping-out* strategy that will take the organisation in a new direction;
- If you're aware that you are a competent player but your future hangs in the balance, you should examine options for a *turnaround* or *survival* strategy. It's resurrection time.
- If your weaknesses and threats are overwhelming and you clearly have no future in the game, you should be designing the most economical *exit* strategy. This is just as important as other forms of strategy, and is often more difficult to execute. However, as we point out in one of our seven principles of strategy: "Above all, strategy is about understanding what you do and don't control, and what is certain and uncertain about the future; and *knowing when to change.*"

It's not necessary for an organisation continually to change its strategy – although it should be regularly reviewed – and so in many strategic conversations the options that are identified are generally tactical options, i.e. the 'how' and the 'what' of achieving the strategic direction that is chosen. These often vary or change as the game evolves due to the divergent tactics of existing or new players; or because of changes in the business environment. As a result, the range of tactical options considered may simply amount to a slight change in the overall game plan. Yet, however slight, that change may be essential. After all, the consistency of a player's game plan can make it vulnerable on account of its predictability to competitors. Then that player loses a measure of competitive edge, and the advantage swings in favour of the other side.

The tactical options formulated in this phase of the strategic conversation should still be somewhat broad, or high level, because if too many smaller, nitty-gritty options are generated they could obfuscate the conversation. Only once these broader options have been explored at the higher level and then converted into decisions, should the 'options within options' be identified. These more practical issues can be addressed at a later stage in an operational planning meeting; or as the conversation model is cascaded through the organisation to departmental level.

The Ethical Compass

Options can however be narrowed down and unpacked further to determine things that can realistically be done within your control. Sometimes options may sound impressive and the answer to an organisation's predicament, but on further analysis they may not be the smartest choice. This is where the interplay between DNA, scope, rules, scenarios and SWOT come back into play. Because descriptive rules of a game are the basic licence to operate. and the normative rules of the game are the moral rules to which any organisation aspiring to be world class should adhere, it makes sense that, for any option to be effective, it must not fall foul of either type of rule. So the direction in which you should point yourself should take cognisance of routes you should avoid just as much as those you ought to follow. We have therefore developed an 'ethical compass' as a guide to action, particularly for those managers who are inclined to check in their values at the office turnstile in favour of power and glory – and money. Think of our compass instead!

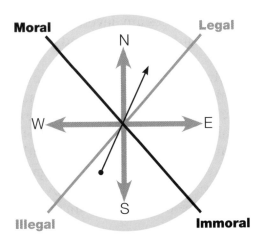

Any option between 'NW' and 'NE' has a reasonable chance of propelling the organisation towards long-term sustainability. However, an option that falls between 'SW' and 'SE' is both immoral and illegal, and will sooner or later prove the undoing of the organisation. We don't like to name any country, leader or organisation in particular that operates in this area, but we all know some that do! The fact is that how you select your options through the ethical compass will unveil what your meaning of winning the game really is.

Given that any organisation has finite resources, options also need to be prioritised on the basis of urgency or importance, leverage (output-to-input ratio), and risk versus reward. Options can sometimes be *exclusive*, meaning you can do either this or that. Normally, the greater the magnitude of resources required the more exclusive the option becomes. Options that provide marginal leverage in the game but do demand high resource input are not great options to choose, and should rather remain in the drawer unless they change their status. Sometimes, though, in order simply to stay in the game in a particular scenario, an option is a prerequisite –

whether or not it provides any leverage at all. In this case it must be converted into a decision, and actioned for defensive reasons.

Choosing exclusive options means refusing others. For an organisation this demands that the opportunity cost of 'the others' must be assessed. Yet, even though life is full of trade-offs, we don't always have to play the trade-off game. Sometimes options are *inclusive* of one another and it's just about choosing the correct set. As long as you design the programme of action in such a way that you're not overstretching your human or financial resources, there are times when you can have it all.

The Treatment of Risk

Often in business, given its similarity to a card game between various players, each incremental step taken in the decision-making chain elicits a change in play and thereby unveils new options, each again with its own risk-reward profile. Hence, playing out the consequences of an option is a critical part of the analysis. Questions should be asked about how the game will change should an option be followed and how the competitors will react. Will it influence the overall business environment? Are there possible hidden risks that could emerge? From a risk-reward perspective, it is like taking bets. It all depends on the magnitude of the bet, the level of risk and your choke limit as a gambler. Very seldom – if ever – in a business situation should an organisation go beyond that magical threshold where too much of the company's destiny is being put on the table. It really doesn't matter how attractive the potential return is, a sensible executive will walk away.

So why take the risk in the first place? Surely if an organisation has been successful in the business offering there's no reason for it to risk changing its strategy? In such a case surely the best option is to do nothing? However, let's not forget that business is a game. Retaining the status quo does not mean that an organisation may continue from here to eternity. Sometimes, on the contrary, continuing to play the game the same way incurs the greatest risk. External factors and a change in the competitors' game plans may suddenly shake the gameboard and topple the organisation into a worst-case scenario. Standing still makes you an easy target.

The final remark we wish to make on risk concerns the 'cautionary principle'. This basically states that where you face a threat, it is wise to take precautions even though the threat may not materialise. It all sounds simple, but the devil is in the detail. We go back to our PI chart because the option of doing something to prevent a nasty thing happening turns on its probability and its potential impact. Nobody disputes taking preventative measures against a terrorist attack (shock event), but the world still does not agree on the measures to be taken to stop climate change (gradual threat). In the end, there is no perfect formula for knowing when to invoke the cautionary principle, how much you should spend and how far you should reduce the odds. It's all about feel. Nevertheless, in areas like the environment, health and safety, options to minimise adverse environmental impacts, reduce the chances of occupational disease and stop accidents that could cause injury and death are receiving much greater attention than before.

It's clear that option generation is on occasion no easy task. Sometimes options are fairly pedestrian, with little risk attached. They just become obvious during the conversation. At other times options are more intricate and perplexing, and may need to be brainstormed in more detail before a decision can be made. They are then held over for further discussion at a subsequent meeting, with an individual or team within the strategy group being tasked to produce draft recommendations by a specified date.

To summarise, the sub-questions we specifically ask to help identify, group and prioritise options are the following:

- What are your strategic and tactical options (i.e. things that you can realistically do within your control) to take the negative scenarios as far as possible out of play, and to thrive in the good ones?
- What options do you need to consider to achieve greater compliance with the rules of the game, specifically the ones to win?
- In relation to the key uncertainties, you have two options: live with them or take them as far as possible out of play. Which choice is realistic for each uncertainty?
- How will the other players in the game react if you pursue the options identified to be the best?
- Are your options in line with your SWOT? In other words, do they add to your competitiveness by exploiting your strengths and reducing your weaknesses; and do they embrace the challenges posed by the opportunities and threats inherent in the game?

We conclude this section with a warning: the process of formulating options may seem a little clearer now, but this stage of the strategic conversation should not be entered into lightly. The most frequent trap for an organisation is to select a change in scope (i.e. strategic direction) and then, because it falls outside the comfort zone of 'business as usual', *not* allocate sufficient resources to make it happen. Business is a complicated and unforgiving game. Clearly identifying the most effective options is one thing. Putting the ones you choose into practice with the intended results is another, especially when you are setting off in a new direction.

Here are some comments which we noted down during this stage of our conversation. Remember that we follow the heuristic method where people are encouraged to discover the best options for themselves in a question and answer mode:

One of the rules in our game is an acute shortage of artisans and other skilled craftsmen, which looks set to continue. A tactical option must therefore be to look at various ways to attract, develop and, especially, retain people of this ilk in our organisation. This demands an overhaul of our personnel policy where such people have up till now been given scant regard compared to, say, recruiting accountants. SENIOR MANAGER, CONSTRUCTION INDUSTRY

Radio as a stand-alone medium is losing ground. The global trend is a shift towards multimedia offerings. If we are to attract new listeners, it is now clear that we need to consider the synergies between the different media platforms. Thus our strategic options are to stay on familiar ground or broaden our offer so that we're seen as a multimedia news and entertainment group, not just a broadcaster. EXECUTIVE, RADIO GROUP

Up till now, we've just given money away to good causes, chosen by our trustees. But, with the advent of public/private partnerships, we must explore the strategic option of partnering with the appropriate level of government to fund desirable projects on a rand-for-rand basis. This represents a major change in direction for the fund with all the risks and complexities associated with having to establish steering committees and the like.
CEO, SOCIAL RESPONSIBILITY FUND

As a provincial law society we play a pivotal role in promoting the legal fraternity within the context of the country's imperatives. A tactical option that has come to the fore, which could give us greater leverage in the game whilst requiring a relatively low resource

input, is that each legal member within our province provides 24 hours' worth of pro bono *work a year to the State (with cases that have been prepared beforehand). Collectively, this allows people who cannot afford legal counsel to receive the service they desperately need; and, at the same time it gives the legal fraternity a different image in the eyes of both the community and, importantly, the government. We may not be as callous as people think!*

HEAD, PROVINCIAL LAW SOCIETY

In the passenger airline industry, routes are critical. Until now we have been beholden to the standard view of maximising the number of routes to give ourselves the greatest reach. It's now increasingly obvious that routing options should be seen from two different angles; one, whether or not they provide long-term strategic advantage; and two, whether they are financially viable. It will be a massive shift for us if we accept the second philosophy, bearing in mind that, when you lose a route, it is very difficult to secure it again. But the state of the market compels us to examine the latter as a strategic option. AIRLINE EXECUTIVE

Our options are to become more transparent in the way we do business; or go on being seen as a secretive tax haven where rich folks can stash their cash. The international net is closing in.

ASSET MANAGER, ISLE OF MAN

We have two strategic options: provide electricity as cheaply as we can to all Indian citizens, or install expensive technology to reduce carbon emissions and raise the price of electricity accordingly. Guess which option wins if America with the highest carbon footprint per citizen in the world refuses to lead the way!

UTILITY EXECUTIVE, NEW DELHI

Your options are limited when the enemy wants to annihilate you.

ISRAELI BUSINESSMAN, JERUSALEM

One option is to do absolutely nothing. Just kidding!

EXECUTIVE, STATIONERY COMPANY

Is it an option for China to evolve into a multiparty democracy as it gets richer? Of course, but let me answer the question with a question: does your company – for which you have worked your entire career in the belief that it is a worthwhile institution – tolerate an official opposition to the Board? No? I rest my case.

CHINESE ACADEMIC, BEIJING

Do you think the option outlined in the 'High Road' scenario of negotiating a settlement with the real opposition leaders is viable? Yes, it is the only road.

INTERCHANGE BETWEEN TWO CABINET MINISTERS,
SCENARIO SESSION ON SOUTH AFRICA, NOVEMBER 1986

Given our diversity as a nation, we need to develop a South Africanness to transcend our differences. Americans are diverse too, but their spirituality, respect for the flag and undoubted economic success have bound them together. They have real national pride – even the minorities. We have the 'High Road' option of fostering our pride or the 'Low Road' option of falling apart.

PARTICIPANT, SCENARIO SESSION, JULY 2007

Thank heavens you put a $70 scenario on the table when the price of oil was $25 a barrel. It scared the living daylights out of us, given that we consume as much energy as a small European country. It made us consider energy-saving options throughout the business and implement solutions where we could. In retrospect, a very wise thing to do. ENERGY HEAD, GLOBAL RESOURCES COMPANY

12 Decisions: Which options do you want to turn into decisions right now, and what is the initial action associated with each decision?

If I am to live longer, perhaps I must live out my old age,
seeing and hearing less, understanding worse, coming to learn
with more difficulty and to be more forgetful, and growing worse
than those to whom I was once superior. Indeed, life would be
unliveable, even if I did not notice the change. And if I see the
change, how could life not be even more wretched and unpleasant?
SOCRATES as quoted by Xenophon in *Memorabilia IV*

Free as air. That's what you are in the previous section when reviewing your options, with the obvious rider that you should be reflecting on your capabilities at the same time. Now comes the sharp end of the conversation when decisions are made, commitments given and actions taken.

Every point, or cross, on our destiny line, and every step we take along it, represents a decision – a moment of action that either keeps us on track or changes our tack. If no decision is made, the result is a hovering moment of indecision, or hesitation, where we are bogged down, remaining in limbo, whilst the game continues unabated around us. The fewer decisions we make, the more uncertain we become. And yet, not making decisions because we feel we do not have sufficient information to make them seems a perfectly rational thing to do. But what is 'sufficient information'? Sometimes, too much information can create such a profusion of possible paths ahead that you are simply too spoilt for choice. Perhaps, like Goldilocks, you don't want your porridge too hot or too cold. You just want the right amount of information.

As you must recognise from our text by now, a decision is never taken in isolation. As a point on your destiny line it represents the convergence of your DNA (which dictates your predisposition to act) with the external events happening in your proximate environment (which are normally outside of your control). Of course, in your imagination and dreams this is not an issue, because you create and control your environment. However, in the real world, decision-making entails juggling the controllable with the uncontrollable and has very real consequences. It should therefore be considered a life skill and not simply an act of choosing the most appealing notion. This is captured wonderfully in a snatch of verse from Dr Seuss's *Oh, the Places You'll Go*. It is one of the few books he wrote for adults as well as children. The extract goes: "Simple it's not, I'm afraid you will find, for a mind-make-upper to make up his mind." The book remains a favourite gift from parents to their sons and daughters upon leaving school and embarking on adulthood. It explores, in entertaining story-book fashion, the very real life skills they must develop in etching out their individual destiny line; in writing their own individual story as a 'mind-make-upper'.

Transferring this line of thinking to the busy and crowded world of business, where decisions often impact significantly on the lives of many, it is critical that companies strengthen their decision-making powers as far as they can. It is only by doing this that they can remain the central character in their own story, the lead player in their own game. Wrong decisions will place companies at the mercy of other players who have taken control of the game; and then such companies will have no alternative but to watch their destiny line being drawn by people who do not have their interests at heart (quite the opposite!). They will be reluctant characters in their own story. Avoidance of the possible pitfalls of incorrect decisions, by engendering a philosophy of covering all eventualities and then waiting to see how a story pans out, won't work either. Straddling a fence can prove very painful! No, this is business; if a profit is to be made, deadlines have to be met and bets placed before the race begins.

The Fall of the Axe

So how do we make the most effective decisions? How do we get to a point where the correct decision becomes clear, where possibly incorrect decisions are discarded and where indecision is a nonevent? We'll try to sketch out the answer, but we have to be truthful and admit that there are no guarantees: you can still make a bad decision through misreading the future or just plain bad luck. At this point of our strategic conversation, keeping an open mind becomes positively counterproductive. Confusion has to be stripped away and a plot of your future destiny line must emerge. Granted, the debate on key uncertainties and alternative futures through scenario construction will hopefully have instilled flexibility in your nature. Granted, challenges to your destiny line may well have been considered and possible contingency plans put in place to change course. But ultimately, the axe has to fall one way or the other for progress to be made and the integrity of your story line to remain intact.

The drama of this moment was expressed towards the end of the conversation between Socrates and the fox. The latter says to Socrates: "So now we come to your question: 'Which option are you going to exercise and turn into action?' Personally I have decided to head north and take my chances there." Socrates enthuses that the conversation has clarified his mind, and unveils his decision to exercise the last option of taking his chances in court. We'd hazard a guess that plenty of people reading this book wouldn't have taken the route of Socrates and risked death. But then, as we now know, Socrates had his reasons; and for him the decision was final.

Some decisions in business are 'no-brainers' and require very little exercising of the grey matter. The key word here is 'some', for the complexity of the game of business inevitably makes most decisions associated with playing the game pretty complicated. Every decision made by management has its outcomes, some expected, others unexpected. But all of them incur reactions to the decision from, on the one hand, the company's own staff playing to their individual needs and acting in their own interests; and on the other hand, from competitors protecting their corners as well. In a way, each decision an organisation makes generates a ripple effect that unsettles a game's status quo and prompts reactions from all sides present on the field. Using the metaphor of 'locker-room talk' before a game, any coach who unveils an unbreakable master plan down to the last detail – thus leaving no room for unanticipated responses from the opposing team – risks losing the game. Taking command of the game demands that players have Plan Bs which can be activated should the reactions of the opposing side demand alternative strategies and tactics. The side's game plan can be adjusted accordingly, keeping the game firmly within their control, but at the same time fluid and unpredictable to the opposition.

Innovative Swans

Applying this metaphor to the game of business, this means, especially in bigger organisations, the more complex the decisions and potential outcomes, the more it is necessary to have the kind of strategic conversation we are outlining – the kind that embraces uncertainty. However, at this point, we must revert to our distinction between strategy and tactics. Strategy, being direction, cannot be chopped and changed at will. One has to be decisive and allow a strategic decision time to bed down and time to validate itself. Tactical decisions, on the other hand, are incremental. Each one can be reviewed to see if it is having the desirable result, and if not the next one can be changed. This bipolar approach to strategy and tactics allows the organisation to have a strategic end-point in mind, while retaining a built-in mechanism for adaptation of tactical decisions as the future unfolds. The incremental philosophy underlying the latter means that an organisation can adjust to a changing environment intuitively and gradually, rather than rashly and overdramatically. Picture a swan gliding serenely through the water. Strategy is what you see on the surface, while tactics are the energetic paddling underneath.

As an added benefit, our process also has innovation built into it. Because the scenario gameboard explores the edge of the envelope in terms of possibilities and opportunities, it promotes innovative thinking and allows new and creative ideas to surface. The thing we find somewhat puzzling is that many major organisations we have worked with treat innovation as a separate entity cloaked in the guise of an 'innovation hub'. It then lives a half life on the outskirts of traditional corporate strategy and every now and then is tapped for any nuggets of creativity that can be moulded into the organisation's official mindset. Unfortunately, when innovation floats around as a disconnected entity from the main decision-making body, most of its ideas are dead in the water.

Innovation doesn't have to be earth-shattering. When Steve Jobs posed to his Apple colleagues the question "Why should all computers be beige?" he wasn't asking for a cataclysmic "Oh wow!" response. It was simply a subtle challenge to the existing state of affairs in the design of personal computers. Yet it proved to be a transformational moment. Moreover, the insights from innovation are not the sole reserve of so-called 'creative thinkers' such as Steve Jobs. In order for an idea or option to be 'innovative', it simply has to offer a departure from an established line of thought. Our conversation model, by going back to basics, encourages such lateral thinking, provided that there is a thoroughness in the depth and scope of its implementation. The more the model is used throughout an organisation, the more inclusive it is, the more iterative it is and the greater the degree of mutual learning and frequency of breakthroughs. It tends to capture the innovation that simmers below the surface of the workforce, which would otherwise go to waste.

The Strategic Statement

As we have just observed but wish to expand on, strategic decisions vary from tactical decisions in that the former define your direction, and relate predominantly to the scope of your game or the definition of your playing field; whereas the latter improve your competitiveness and thereby your organisation's position in the game you have selected. A strategic decision can therefore lead to a change in range of products or services; repositioning within the product chain; an entry into a new market segment and/or an expansion of the geographical footprint. Sometimes it can lead to a change in the game altogether, should the current one be unplayable. Sometimes, it confirms that there is no need for any shift in direction, in which case the decisions made are exclusively tactical.

Given the critical importance of an organisation's strategic direction, we become somewhat alarmed if it becomes evident early on in the conversation that an organisation's strategy is not fully written up in one particular place. All too often the strategic model is fragmented, its elements scattered about in different forms and in different parts of the organisation. This naturally undermines the purpose and results in limited buy-in. No defined goalposts mean no clear playing field and no nets to aim the ball at. It is therefore paramount that the first decision should take the form of a synthesis of the outcomes of the strategic conversation concerning the organisation's future scope. The latter should be expressed in a pithy statement which has a dynamic ring about it so that it can be presented as the vision of the organisation – an internal communication tool to rally the troops. At least each business unit or department can then build its strategies and tactics in line with the organisation's central strategy. The playing field is clearly marked and the goalposts are upright for all to see. It also gives the strategic process a simple, clean end-point that enables effective activations along the way.

Incremental Tactics

Once this strategic statement had been formulated, it is easier to go back to the options and convert them into decisions. Indeed, we often juxtapose options with decisions, because frequently the only decision that can be made at the time is to explore the option more fully. On other occasions, the decision may be to defer the option until resources become available or circumstances warrant its pursuit. Where a decision is taken to implement an option, the initial action to get the show on the road must be described and assigned to whoever in the team is considered most suitable. In this sense, the process should be incremental, with further steps being agreed upon after the first step is complete. This keeps everyone on the ball and allows continual monitoring of the implementation programme. The concept we are advocating is evident in the game of golf, where many a professional will invariably answer the question as to how he or she is going to play the game with "One shot at a time". You'll be surprised how enthusiastic people can be in ensuring the implementation of their actions when they're being measured incrementally and they have a deadline for each incremental step! Any excuse about the complexity of the task delaying the project sounds pretty lame in these circumstances.

In summary, sub-questions we often ask when going through the decision-making stage of our model are the following:

- What is your strategic intent and direction?
- What are the preferred options that, right now, are 'go' and can be turned into decisions and actions?
- What is the initial action associated with each decision; i.e. who is going to do what by when and how much is it going to cost? (Sometimes there is no additional cost because it is just extra workload for an existing team member.)
- What options do you want to defer, either because they are lower priority or will only be triggered by other scenarios coming into play?
- Which options are too risky or unethical and should therefore be rejected as possible decisions?
- Where an option is exclusive, has the decision to take it been weighed up against the 'opportunity cost' of refusing all the other options?
- What, if any, are the potentially unintended and undesirable consequences associated with the decisions?

At this point in the book you should realise that you have two options: write your own story and determine your own destiny line, or let others do it for you. Although Socrates' decision to place his life in the hands of the courts was made with the full knowledge of what the outcome might possibly be, he never abandoned his destiny line; and although he left it to others to write his story, he had an inkling of the theme and the finale. But then he was Socrates – the father of modern philosophy. Meanwhile, the fox took his chances in the forest. For the rest of us, if we are to write our own stories, the next decision should be to finish the book and learn how to identify the outcomes we desire.

Here is a sample of the decisions made by companies and other organisations for which we have worked:

Because the game has become increasingly difficult, our decision is to niche ourselves and focus on the ultra-premium sector. The logic is that this sector is less vulnerable to economic cycles because the rich will always have money to drink. We in turn will have more control of our destiny. WINEMAKER

As a clothing retailer supplying the lower-to-middle income market we have access to, and knowledge of, consumers with whom other industries can create huge marketing opportunities. Our decision is to move into selling 'pay-as-you-go' airtime for mobile telephones, which will open up a whole new, and highly profitable, business unit for us. In fact, it should surpass our core business. Our ambition is to become the single largest customer for the cellular service providers. Their decisions around this market will come from our knowledge base and customer understanding. Of course the next decision will revolve around how to play in two games at the same time. DIRECTOR, MASS-MARKET CLOTHING RETAILER

Currently, my raw materials cost more than the landed cost of a Chinese suit or shirt. I could pay my workers nothing and I still couldn't compete. This conversation has convinced me to go to the higher ground of tailoring suits and shirts for the individual needs of customers. And I'll import the rest of my requirements from China. CEO, CLOTHING MANUFACTURER

As a result of the attention given to auditing firms following the Enron scandal, many professional firms made the decision to split their services. We have decided to keep all our services under one brand, but we will erect 'Chinese walls' between them. CEO, FINANCIAL SERVICES FIRM

After your session, we decided to marry a foreign gorilla to expand our African footprint. What a good strategic move! EXECUTIVE, LEADING BANKING GROUP

168

Our sales team are losing ground with our customers because they are playing a traditional marketing game. However, marketing now demands a more strategic focus and closer alignment with the operational side of the business. Having decided to change the internal rules of the game, our key decision is to build new competencies into the sales team. Training and internal communication are critical for us. These decisions are purely tactical because we want to keep our scope the same.   DIRECTOR, PRINTING COMPANY

The first thing we shall do after this session is articulate the golden rules to win the game and brief all our staff. We shall also introduce key performance indicators (KPIs) for each of the rules and measure performance against them. Finally, we'll make the KPIs an integral part of our remuneration system by attaching financial incentives for the staff to achieve them. In other words, we'll take the golden rules as seriously as any American company and thereby sharpen our competitiveness. It should keep us in the top half of your business gameboard.   CEO, SOFTWARE HOUSE

We're definitely going to introduce a talent-management system in light of the rule about attracting, developing and retaining talented staff. It means hiring a human resource person, but that's no bad thing since we've always given that discipline short shrift.

MD, ASSET-MANAGEMENT BUSINESS

Our decision has to be that we should be seen as the best head-hunting outfit in Africa. We will need a database containing the names of all CEOs and CFOs in every African country, as well as the names of all expatriates from the continent in those positions wherever they may be around the world.

SENIOR PARTNER, HEAD-HUNTING BUSINESS

Our decision is to go into Africa and brand ourselves as African rather than South African. It will produce some interesting reac-

tions from our global competitors. However, our decision on which countries to enter will be based on careful analysis of each country's market and prospects.   DIRECTOR, FAST-FOOD COMPANY

The decision has already been taken to re-integrate Taiwan into the Middle Kingdom. The only question is on what terms and when. We can wait a hundred years.   CHINESE STRATEGIST, BEIJING

Definitely the biggest takeaway from this session is that we need to expand our donor base and retain the services of a full-time professional fundraiser in order to make it happen.

DIRECTOR, HIV / AIDS FOUNDATION

The most important issue raised in this workshop is the level of intellectual leadership we should be giving on the major environmental issues of the day – such as global warming, marine conservation and management of elephant herds in game parks. We are already involved in a number of projects in these areas, but we need to be more visible in championing the causes and educating the public on viable solutions. Let it be so.

CHAIRMAN, GLOBAL ENVIRONMENTAL AGENCY

We got the young talent in the company to sit around a table and use your conversation model to give their views on the company's future. Boy, were their recommendations different to our decisions!

CHAIRMAN, EXECUTIVE COMMITTEE OF ENTERTAINMENT GROUP

Today's conversation has convinced me that we need to get a better handle on the long-term trends in recidivism (relapse) of our patients in order to judge the effectiveness of our treatments. I think we would be pleasantly surprised by the results in regard to alcohol abuse, but mortified by the lack of success with drug addiction.

CEO, LEADING REHABILITATION CLINIC

13 Outcomes: What is your meaning of winning the game in five years' time, expressed as a set of measurable outcomes?

*Our purpose in founding the city was not to make
any one class in it surpassingly happy, but to make the
city as a whole as happy as possible.*
SOCRATES, as quoted by Plato in *The Republic.*

If we are guilty of a presumption in writing this book, it is that ordinary human beings play the game to win. Only masochists prefer to lose. But here's the key question: what, for you, is 'winning'? What is *your* 'meaning' of winning the game? To make as much money as possible, as quickly as possible? To beat the other guy? To be number one in the game for as long as possible? To be a legend? To lead an anonymous but happy life, balancing your career with family and recreational pursuits? To make a difference in *other* people's lives? To be a hedonist and seek pleasure for pleasure's sake? In today's world, the last question would attract a host of affirmative answers with which Socrates would definitely not agree.

If you think winning is only about chasing targets then you've already lost the game. It's easy to circle a point on a graph and say: "That's our end-point, that's where we want to be: now, team, let's get there." Indeed, we made just this assertion in the last chapter when advocating that management draw up a strategic statement before getting down to tactics. But if the chase becomes too blinkered, you will invariably lose sight of what else is happening around you and of the shifts in the game that can throw you off course. The true meaning of winning should be bigger than merely chasing a collective target. It should be about each individual identifying his or her real purpose in the game; why he or she has chosen the game and what he or she wants the outcomes to be. Not for one moment are we suggesting that this marvellous diversity of human nature be reflected in the strategic statement. It would become too long and too nuanced. But what we are implying is that the conversation will be the poorer for not permitting the diversity of opinion about the yardsticks for success to be revealed before the conversation closes. Those around the table must have their say on this matter.

The Meaning of Success

We have intentionally left the question of winning until last on the grounds that it can only really be answered once you have understood the game, and your role in it. Being contrarian like Socrates, we have gone against the grain of contemporary thinking in doing this. Most strategic methodologies demand that an organisation's purpose and meaning of success should be addressed first in order to set the agenda for the rest of the discussion. We, on the other hand, want to keep the debate as open-ended as possible for as long as possible, with the first moment of alignment coming with the strategic statement of the last section. The latter constitutes a perfect stepping stone to a deeper discussion on the game's proper meaning and direction. One of the chief objectives of this final session is to construct a series of indicators to tell you whether or not you're on course for a desirable future – as *you* desire it.

In their dialogue, Socrates asks the fox what he considers to be the 'meaning of life'; to which the fox replies: "I suppose it has to do with the reproduction of my species. That is my legacy. I have to protect my wife and children so that someday in some distant country my several times great-grandchildren will carry on the foxy tradition." 'Legacy' is also foremost in Socrates' mind when he concurs with the fox about leaving something behind. In his case, his fervent wish was that his idea of enquiry persisted in the minds of future generations. The fox's next observation highlighted the paradox for Socrates: "In all probability, that will happen if you suffer the worst of all possible fates." Eternal fame for Socrates was linked to his premature death.

Luckily for us, the chances are that we will never be called upon to leave our mark on the world through the dilemma that faced Socrates. Emerging battered and bruised is probably the worst possible fate for most of us! Business is a tough game, as is life, but for many human beings it constitutes a major dimension of their existence. Although their respective DNAs impinge on the way they play the business game, it is the unpredictable nature of the game itself that gives it complexity, and shapes their experiences. This complexity is not so common in the game of sport where 'winning' is clearly expressed on a scoreboard or scorecard at the end of a finite period of play. Someone wins, someone loses, or there is a draw; or (as in golf) there is a list of who came where when the event is over.

By contrast, the changing nature of business is relentless and unforgiving; sustainability has no time frame and no end; therefore there's no clear moment when you can announce an overall winner. If a corporate competitor falls, another will be there to pick up the baton, and their very presence will change the game. Therefore, should you wish to 'win' in the game, you have to determine what it *means* for you to win; within your time frames and according to your own personal criteria for success. Coming third in a race, for example, could be a win for you if the previous year the best you could do was seventh; and provided that coming third falls in line with your sequential plan for improvement.

Let's shift the analogy for a minute. Imagine you've seen your reflection in the mirror, winced and made the decision to lose a little weight. You're going to play the 'weight' game. In order to measure your progress you naturally think it best to set a target weight and keep an eye on the scale. Is this an accurate measurement of winning? Not really. It is in fact quite disempowering at times because it only measures short-term shifts in your body weight. It also relies predominantly on tactics. It is, after all, quite possible to lose weight quite dramatically using extreme tactics, but at the expense of good health. The true meaning of winning the weight game would therefore have to include assessments of body tone and overall health. These would provide the necessary components of a longer-term, more sustainable win than simply the loss of weight as measured by the scales. It's all about seeing the bigger picture of the game (not of yourself, hopefully). Otherwise, you will put it all on again!

A Measured Balance

Defining a well-balanced meaning of winning is both an empowering and uplifting experience, and a nice way to end the conversation on a positive note. This applies in every sector of business. We have chosen five years as a suitable period to focus the mind – anything less being too short and anything beyond beginning to appear too long. Who knows what the world will be like in ten to twenty years' time? Although it is undeniably the collective responsibility of the executive committee/board of directors to determine strategic direction, the organisation that is expected to embrace it will always be a social organisation made up of different people with different wishes and opinions, different strengths and weaknesses, different aspirations and values. There is no single meaning of winning. A successful strategy is one that is articulated through a balance of the different meanings of winning. Instead of one person placing one point on the graph and saying "right, let's get there", a more meaning-ful expression of intent for the organisation would be one where the strategic statement of the last chapter is supplemented by a series of agreed outcomes which map out the organisation's destiny line in the foreseeable future. Such outcomes represent a composite of the individual ambitions of the executives for the company, i.e. where they would personally like to see it going. And that brings substance to the purpose of the game.

We achieve this objective by posing the question at the start of the chapter to each member of the strategy team – perhaps rephrasing it thus: "What is your personal criterion by which you will judge whether the company has won or lost the game in, say, five years' time?" Predictably, each member of the team will have a different answer. For example, the director of human resources may well state that the meaning of winning for him consists of being the employer of choice in the industry, and thereby one to which the top graduates in the field will turn first when looking for a job. Indeed, he may add that one of the rules to win is about developing talented people to the point where they act as key differentiators. Having the pick of graduate talent is therefore a good foundation for a sustainable victory. From another perspective, the technical director, with an eye on retaining the company's profile as an organisation on the cutting edge, will probably want at least three revolutionary breakthroughs in product design during the five years. And so on. The 'meaning of winning' for the company is thus balanced in the sense that no one meaning of winning predominates over another to the point where the 'whole meaning' is impaired. Of course, all this somehow has to fall into line with the CEO's passionate desire to elevate the share price (because he or she inevitably has more share options than anyone else!).

We know what you're thinking: surely working with too

many meanings of winning can very well prove confusing and diffuse the value of the process? The point has validity, but balancing these meanings of winning is not impossible. The secret is to work with four or five *key* meanings of winning by clustering the answers from the strategy team. In this way, by the end of the process, each member of the team feels that they have contributed their money's worth, and the result is a *balanced scorecard* which, with the strategic statement as a precursor, can be treated as the overall mission statement for the company for the next five years. It represents a concrete expression of the purpose and subsidiary goals of the entire company, and incidentally serves as a much more useful tool than the biblical homilies which usually pass for the corporate 'vision' in the annual report.

As far as possible, meanings of winnings should consist of measurable outcomes. So instead of recording your wish as: "To be a company people want to work for" (perfectly healthy but unmeasurable), the statement should read: "To be included in the Top 10 of so-and-so's published list of companies to work for." The obvious advantage of having a measurable outcome is that it is a definitive goal which demands accountability on the part of the person or persons who are entrusted with the challenge of championing that element of the organisation's purpose.

Having such a balanced meaning of winning recognises that business is a considerably more subtle pastime than sport. As already intimated, there is no ultimate winner, no outright victory, because the game never stops. Yet another dimension is that, although the purpose of business is to win, it should not necessarily be to make other people lose. Sometimes an organisation must accept a 'draw', on the grounds that an outright victory would have repercussions that could scupper the game completely, taking the organisation down with it. Monopolies are frowned upon! Equally, a balanced game is one in which the impacts of certain uncontrollable factors are, to some degree, shared by all the players and perhaps mitigated by their collective influence. For instance, what is the purpose of business chambers other than to do this? Upsetting the balance of a game can mean opening it up to the unchecked ravages of alien factors and alien players. In practice, business is therefore a combination of pure rivalry and co-operative games which requires a very delicate balance between the two. We like to think of it as a touch of von Neuman with a dash of Nash (the two mathematicians who excelled in the field of game theory).

Summing up, we are well aware of the argument that if you chase two rabbits you will catch neither. This is often used to justify why it's a good idea to focus on one target at a time and go for it. We argue that if you're clever in your use of lettuce, both rabbits will *come to you*. Defining your organisation's purpose upfront limits the richness of the debate by constricting thought, discouraging new insights and narrowing the options. It is only satisfactory if your organisation is intent on spending a short time in the game, taking a short cut to success. But if your organisation is looking towards a more epic journey, where its presence as a business leader will be felt far and wide and its legacy will be experienced long after it may have left the playing field, it needs constantly to reinvent itself as the game changes. This requires open debate of the highest order, with maximum participation.

Socrates debated issues throughout his life without ever abandoning his characteristic humility. The fact that his non-acceptance of things at face value is still the guiding philosophy of many of the world's greatest scientists and philosophers, so long after his death, is the result of the balance he achieved in his meaning of winning. His choice to accept the worst possible fate so that his idea of enquiry would warrant sufficient respect to be remembered by future generations was a defining moment. There are many great philosophers, but Socrates will always stand alone because of that. As humans, our attention is drawn to the point in any story that defines it, that gives it purpose, and that ensures its longevity in the minds of those who have been absorbed by it. So, we must ask you now: what is your innermost thought on the purpose of your organisation? What is the story you would like to see unfold? What is the 'win' you desire?

We conclude this chapter with some provocative definitions on the meaning of winning the game:

The meaning of winning in our business would be to achieve the following measurable outcomes in the next five years:
- *to have a supply chain excellence programme in place whereby we have forged closer and more productive links with our key suppliers;*
- *to be considered the 'supplier of choice' in our annual customer survey by at least eight out of our top ten customers;*
- *to have opened businesses in at least three other African countries and to be generating at least 20 per cent of our revenue from these sources;*
- *to continue to grow our bottom-line profit at 25 per cent per annum, the rate we have achieved over the last five years; and*
- *to be voted by our employees as the best company to work for in the published survey of our industry.*

EXECUTIVE TEAM, COMPONENT MANUFACTURER

Our meaning of winning in five years can be expressed in three simple outcomes. Just to have made progress will be good enough. The outcomes are:
- *to halve the HIV/AIDS prevalence rate in the community in which we work by the introduction of effective prevention programmes;*

- *to have full coverage in terms of home-based care for households affected by the epidemic; and*
- *to ensure that the clinical capability exists to test all those that want to be tested and to provide antiretroviral drugs to all those who need to be treated.*   DIRECTOR, HIV/AIDS NGO

We will have won the game in five years if we can do at least two things:
- *continue to be as competitive as the best New Zealand dairy farms by adopting global best practice and even improving on it where we can; and*
- *turn the business into a model for black economic empowerment that can be used elsewhere in the farming industry.*

DAIRY FARMER, EASTERN CAPE, SOUTH AFRICA
(who subsequently won the award for the empowerment deal of the year from a major bank)

My contribution to the meaning of winning is to create an environment within which the majority of our employees become our brand champions because they are so proud of working for our company.

MD, CLOTHING MANUFACTURER AND RETAILER

For me, the meaning of winning is when the human resources division is recognised by line management as a strategic business partner in this company.   HEAD OF HUMAN RESOURCES, MULTIMEDIA GROUP

In this game, one of the critical meanings of winning is to triple our current reserves within five years. Another is to improve our health and safety statistics by at least 20 per cent per annum.

EXECUTIVE, GOLD-MINING GROUP

The reality is that we can't begin to win the game if we don't achieve our objective of raising R500 million over five years. But it's not just about the money. We need to use that money to make huge inroads

into providing tertiary education for thousands of people in Africa who would not otherwise get it. We want to be the biggest and best distance-learning institution on the continent, however that is measured.   HEAD, UNIVERSITY FOUNDATION

For me, winning means each agent selling on average 1.5 houses per month and the company having the largest waiting list of agents because it is seen as the market leader.

SENIOR MANAGER, LEADING RESIDENTIAL PROPERTY GROUP

For the people of China, the meaning of winning is to become the largest economy in the world (again) by 2040. But we can't do that at the expense of the environment; which is why in our latest five-year plan we have a target of reducing energy consumption per unit of GDP by 20 per cent.   CHINESE ECONOMIST, BEIJING

Our preparatory school has been established for almost a hundred years; but our high school is new. Our meaning of winning is to see the two integrated into a well-respected educational institution spanning the most important years of a child's life. We would also like to be seen as representative of people from every kind of background, which means establishing a significant bursary/scholarship fund and having active alumni who participate fully in our development programmes.   HEADMASTER, INDEPENDENT BOYS' HIGH SCHOOL

In a nutshell, our meaning of winning is to get through the next five years without any major incidents of power outages or voluntary/ involuntary load-shedding. We want to be seen by our prime customers as a strategic partner of choice.   EXECUTIVE, PARASTATAL

If ever we introduce a container deposit system in Western Australia, the criteria for judging whether we've won the game in five to ten years' time will be that:

- *an improvement in container recovery rates to a level of*

180

80 per cent is achieved within two years of inception and maintained thereafter;

- *manufacturers significantly redesign their products so that they are better suited to recycling;*
- *the system is cost-effective and self-funding;*
- *state government and industry begin to work together to solve the problem of waste avoidance; and*
- *the mindset of consumers towards the environment changes because they feel empowered to do something about it.*

PANEL OF EXPERTS, WASTE MANAGEMENT WORKSHOP,
FREMANTLE, AUSTRALIA

A measurable outcome which would indicate we're winning our game is to be the organiser of 15 large-scale events a year – ones that repeat themselves either because the topic is evergreen or because it's an annual industry conference. CEO, CONFERENCE ORGANISER

My meaning of winning? Hmm. Like your fox, I treat life incrementally – one day at a time. I guess being the man in the White House in five years' time would be nice! If not, I'll find other ways to win the game. EX-US MAYOR, AFRICAN HR SUMMIT, JOHANNESBURG

The meaning of winning for a goalkeeper is to stop the other side from scoring goals. The meaning of winning for a striker is to score goals. Stopping something happening is not nearly as glamorous as making something happen. That's why strikers are much better known than goalkeepers. But I suppose the same applies to anybody in the prevention game. Heaven forbid you should let something through. The sky falls on your head. EX-MANCHESTER UNITED
GOALKEEPER, CO-PRESENTER, AUDITING CONFERENCE

In defining the criteria for South Africa to become a 'winning nation', I'm sure the people around this table will give you quite different answers. After all, we are a democracy. But for the 'meaning

of losing', you only have to look north to Zimbabwe. It is our 'cautionary tale'.

PARTICIPANT, SCENARIO WORKSHOP ON SOUTH AFRICA

We had a memorable session at which all the players in the game bird industry – the conservationists, the farmers, the shooters and the safari operators – were present. Not only did we achieve a better understanding of the overall game, we also clearly defined our respective roles in winning it. It also made us realise that to play a leading role as a research organisation, we needed a full-time CEO. One of the participants at the session applied for and got the job and we've never looked back.

CHAIRMAN, GAME BIRD RESEARCH NGO

For us, a yardstick for winning is to continue to be voted the second-best managed port in Africa – or even the best. We also want to maintain our status as a principal gateway for trade into southern Angola. CFO, NAMIBIAN PORTS AUTHORITY, WALVIS BAY

Winning is Living with a capital 'L'. Losing is Dying without Living. DEEJAY, LEADING HIP-HOP RADIO STATION, JOHANNESBURG

We're about to be hit by a tsunami of cash arriving from the exploitation of our oil and gas fields. Billions upon billions of extra dollars rolling into the government exchequer every year. Like the winner of the largest lottery on earth, we can spend the money wisely or foolishly. Winning is the first option.

OFFICIAL, GOVERNMENT OF AZERBAIJAN

The meaning of winning is catching the fox.
MEMBER OF BRITISH ROYAL FAMILY, AWARDS CEREMONY, CAPE TOWN

EPILOGUE

14 From Socrates to Wack: Looking Forward and Looking Back

Often when looking at a mass of things for sale, he would say to himself, "How many things I have no need of!"
DIOGENES LAERTIUS on Socrates in *Lives of the Eminent Philosophers*

Traditional ways of formulating strategy have their place, but they also have their weaknesses; and in the face of growing uncertainty in the world, those weaknesses are not the foundations upon which organisations should plan for the future. However, many organisations seem reluctant to change their linear approach towards strategy, and are attracted instead to the seductively easy conclusions that such an approach brings.

Imagine if strategy could be so straightforward that data could be fed into a computer model and then a future would pop out of the other end for every one to digest and plan around accordingly. Such a model existed for the oil industry as far back as the early 1970s. After crunching data involving 120 variables, the model produced the seemingly unassailable prediction that the world would run out of oil within twenty years. It was clearly wrong.

East Meets West

But someone did get it right. Incontestably so in fact. His name was Pierre Wack, and he was anything but typical. He was a French economist with a flair for Indian mysticism. He had studied under George Gurdjieff, a religious philosopher who brought to the West a mystic tradition within Islam known as Sufism. Amongst other things Wack learnt from Gurdjieff was the value of 'seeing' as performed by mystics, and that the true secret of the martial arts was the ability to 'see' when an opponent was about to strike and therefore when and where to strike or retaliate with maximum effect. As Wack described it: "Naturally, we 'look' with our minds – with interpretations, inferences, perceptions, comparisons, expectations, and through all our previous experiences. Actually, to 'see' is a function of a pure consciousness. It is an enchantment." In other words, cut out all those filters that cloud your everyday observations and judgement. Link your senses directly to your soul.

Later Wack would travel to Svamiji's ashram in India to learn more about this practice "of not believing, imagining, speculating, but seeing". He admitted that he was not 'predisposed' to see but was more inclined to give himself over to 'interpretation' and 'mental constructions'. As such he likened the challenge of his conversion to splitting an old, tough tree trunk with an axe, the tree being 'knotty' and with 'lots of curious difficulties'. "Svamiji", he said, "was without equal when it came to discovering the right angle of attack, coming up with an adequate axe and inspiring his disciple with the will to use it, because in this case, the disciple was both the trunk and the one who has to use the axe."

Wack's affinity for Indian mysticism seemed out of place in the early 1970s in the dour corporate corridors of Royal Dutch/Shell in London where he was part of a new division called Group Planning. But it helped him separate himself and the group from the traditional forecasting techniques used at the time, and move towards a new approach of handling the future called 'scenario planning' – or, as Wack preferred to call it, 'scenario thinking'. The latter, as he explained, "demands, firstly, the identification of the forces at work and the chain(s) of cause and effect behind the development of a market; and, secondly, information about a chain that is much wider than global statistics, a ladder where significant differences appear". He did not invent scenario planning. That accolade belongs to Herman Kahn, an American genius who served as a consultant to the US armed forces and even wrote a bestseller on military scenarios with the title *On Thermonuclear War: Thinking About the Unthinkable.* Indeed, Wack was a student of Kahn. Yet his achievement is still monumental, for he took a discipline which was created in a military setting and adapted it to commerce.

Under Wack's guidance, Shell designed scenarios through which they managed to 'see' possible futures for the price of oil and what forces could affect it; and when the seemingly 'unthinkable' oil price shock came in October 1973, only Shell had captured it in a scenario. But as Wack was wont to say on many occasions afterwards, that was not enough. "Svamiji had made it very clear to me that it wasn't only important to see, but also to make others see. Without this, scenarios which went so much against the ruling expectations of the day would be nothing but 'water on the stone', that would dissipate without leaving a trace." Indeed, he was bitterly disappointed that the scenario did not penetrate the 'microcosm' of Shell decision-makers to the point that it changed their minds on strategy. They did nothing.

He then spent the next few years plying each senior executive with questions in order to understand how to connect to them and what language to use. When the second oil price shock happened in the late 1970s, he anticipated it with a scenario that captured their imagination because of the homework he had done. This time they acted by building up their oil stocks in advance; and almost overnight Shell moved from being one of the smaller of the seven large oil companies in the world to becoming the second biggest. The Gallic guru had passed the Wack test!

Just as Socrates is widely considered as being the 'father' of Western philosophy, so is Pierre Wack thought of as the 'elder statesman' of scenario planning; and he is widely credited for laying the foundations for scenario thinking in business, still one of the most successful (though alas not yet mainstream) forms of strategising for the future. Wack's distinctive approach to scenarios was a fascinating combination of deep perception and intellect, often resulting in profound insight. He believed that this acute perception of the future – or 'reperception' – came about by freeing oneself from old perceptions and prejudices. "Taking off the blinkers", he called it, "and taking on the peripheral vision of a racehorse." You could then pick up the 'strong tendencies' of the present which acted as constraints on the future in important ways. An alternative name he gave to these forces was 'predetermined elements', and the example he often quoted was the monsoon rains that subsequently cause floods on the plains of the Ganges downstream. It has to happen. By sheer concentration, backed up by systematic application of logic or reasoning, he felt that you could peel away the layers of uncertainty and move from uncertainty-based – or, as he called them, 'first-generation' – scenarios and create 'second-generation' scenarios that were a lot more than an imaginary projection; they were a window onto the future.

The Socratic Link

Sound familiar? Even though Pierre Wack was considered a visionary, his driving philosophy was hardly new. Over two thousand years before Wack, Socrates was explaining to his students that true wisdom could only come about by returning to first principles and vigorously questioning them. Any answers that were provided were not the real answers but were masked by the influence of established beliefs and norms and should be considered preludes to further, deeper questioning. By steadily identifying and eliminating those hypotheses that led to contradiction, Socrates

187

gave his students the ability to reperceive the world around them.

Wack also spoke of hypotheses, and often quoted Roberta Wohlsletter, the famous historian of military intelligence who attributed the failure of the US forces to anticipate an attack on Pearl Harbour to their lack of considering a variety of hypotheses outside the realm of contemporary thinking. We sympathise with this view, having had our analysis of a massive terrorist attack on the West fall on deaf ears prior to 9/11 (see the letter to the US president in *The Mind of a Fox* published by Human & Rousseau and Tafelberg in June 2001). Furthermore, Wack believed that the formation of scenarios encouraged participants to sharpen their focus on the key environmental considerations surrounding any business, aided by a deeper and richer language system through which ideas and data could be exchanged.

The similarities between Socrates and Wack don't end there. Both provided a way of thinking that produces an empowering conversation amongst those tasked with creating policy. Limits are tested and radical departures from the norm countenanced. For Wack, this opened up new possibilities which he considered the driving forces behind entrepreneurial flair and foresight. In a similar vein, Socratic dialogue forces participants to re-examine their own belief and value systems and, where necessary, revise them. Wack spoke of an 'inner space', where participants are obliged to question their assumptions about how their business world works and, where necessary, re-organise or change their inner models of reality. This he contrasted with the 'outer space' beyond the control of the participants and subject to rigorous scenario analysis (and possible reperception).

Both Socrates and Wack rocked their worlds. Through his relentless pursuit of virtue and truth, and as a social and moral critic of the Athenian status quo, Socrates challenged

188

not only the city's authority but also its whole way of life. By irritating the establishment with his interrogations of the common man's meaning of justice and goodness, he suffered the ultimate injustice of being tried for supposedly corrupting the youth, and was sentenced to death. Pierre Wack fascinated the establishment with his hooded eyes, goatee beard and the incense he liked to breathe in before uttering something controversial. He actually looked quite like Socrates (or rather what we believe Socrates looked like). But above all, it was his appeal to mystical philosophy that rattled the grey suits together with his uncanny ability to 'see' things they didn't.

Just as Socrates' thinking attracted a dedicated core of deep-thinking, dynamic intellectuals; so it alienated him from mainline popular thought. To a lesser extent, Pierre Wack's approach to business strategy was cold-shouldered by established business thinkers; but his unrivalled success in the field earned him the respect and following of some of the most original and insightful minds in business. In fact, the team that followed in his footsteps at Royal Dutch/Shell and developed his work foresaw the rise of Mikhail Gorbachev and the collapse of Communism years before these events were on anybody else's radar screen.

But in a world where business leaders demand quick-fix solutions based on computer models and quantified predictions, the embracing of uncertainty as recommended by scenario thinking proved too unfamiliar to take off as a tool for business strategy. Consequently, only the exceptional and more forward-thinking companies followed Pierre Wack's philosophy of strategising. Moreover, it was only towards the end of his life that scenario thinking really got its second breath, most notably in South Africa where it is not an exaggeration to suggest that his methodology influenced a nation's destiny. As he remarked to one of us at the time: "Changing the mindset of a company is one thing: changing the mindset of a nation – *c'est magnifique.*" Tragically, it took his death in 1997 to make it clear to the world that it had lost one of its least-known but most remarkable business thinkers.

Coincidentally, the true power of Socrates' philosophy was only fully appreciated after his death (like the paintings of Vincent van Gogh). Yet little is known of him directly from his own words, as he never wrote anything. Instead, what knowledge we have of him comes from the testimony of others. Even as death approached, he never lost his moral integrity. His last words were reputed to be a request to settle an outstanding debt: "Crito, we owe a cock to Aesculapius; please pay it and don't let it pass." Both he and Pierre Wack have often been described as 'remarkable' men. But they were humble too.

The End of the Beginning

And so it is that, as active and passionate proponents of scenario thinking, we have embodied the principles of both Socrates and Pierre Wack into our work. Like the fox, we have been *resourceful* and adapted our model with experience. We have used the Socratic method in a deep and rigorous process to challenge the basic beliefs of the important decision-makers; to integrate intuition with logic; to demand that participants look both inwards and outwards; to use scenarios to create windows onto the future; and finally to make people *act* on the practical implications of the scenarios.

In addition, we have also tried to steer the thinking of participants in our sessions towards the sometimes unpalatable realities of change and to address the often tumultuous world of intensifying competition, unstoppable advances in technology, abrupt turnarounds in economic cycles, and shifting allegiances between nations. Our process is succinct; and it uses a time frame for the conversation that is acceptable in today's world, where pressing issues from all quarters demand the effective use of time. It deals with facts as well as perceptions. It enables continual additions and updates as the future turns into the past. Yet, it steadfastly remains true to the philosophy of scenario thinking, which is to provide a unique competence to the players in today's uncertain game of business.

Pierre Wack said of scenarios that they serve two main purposes. The first is proactive – anticipating and understanding risk; the second is entrepreneurial – discovering strategic options of which we were previously unaware. For many people in business and other activities, the kind of game-playing which underlies our model is something which they may find strange. But as most of the executive teams whose sessions we have facilitated will attest, it is not that difficult to master. Our questions do not intrude on discussing the real business. Quite the reverse.

Socrates said of education: it is the kindling of a flame, not the filling of a vessel, that counts. We hope that we have stoked a fire within you, and that you are ready to adopt our approach by answering our ten questions. We have said our bit. The rest is now up to you. Or, as the fox would say: "Now that the conversation has ended, so may the journey begin." Your destiny line stretches ahead.